I0139327

Unreconciled

Unreconciled

The New Norm

Paul S. Jeon

WIPF & STOCK · Eugene, Oregon

UNRECONCILED
The New Norm

Copyright © 2018 Paul S. Jeon. All rights reserved. Except for brief quotations in critical publications or reviews, no part of this book may be reproduced in any manner without prior written permission from the publisher. Write: Permissions, Wipf and Stock Publishers, 199 W. 8th Ave., Suite 3, Eugene, OR 97401.

Wipf & Stock
An Imprint of Wipf and Stock Publishers
199 W. 8th Ave., Suite 3
Eugene, OR 97401

www.wipfandstock.com

PAPERBACK ISBN: 978-1-5326-5593-7
HARDCOVER ISBN: 978-1-5326-5594-4
EBOOK ISBN: 978-1-5326-5595-1

Manufactured in the U.S.A.   OCTOBER 17, 2018

To James Forsyth,

Preacher, Leader, Friend

Contents

Acknowledgments | *ix*

Introduction | *xi*

1   Identity (Philemon 1–3, 23–25) | 1

2   Community (Philemon 4–7) | 17

3   Peacemaking (Philemon 8–22) | 37

Epilogue | 56

Appendix: Translation and Notes | 59

Bibliography | 65

Acknowledgments

FIRST, I THANK BRIAN Forman whose diligence and love for Jesus inspire many. Without his efforts, the production of this book would have been delayed indefinitely. Second, I thank Garret and Grace Djeu whose commitment to facilitate peace illustrates much of what I discuss in this book. Finally, I thank my wife who responds to all my inadequacies with love and grace.

Introduction

THOUGH BRIEF, PAUL'S LETTER to Philemon is rich in meaning, reminding Christians of the importance of reconciliation, mediation, and winsome persuasion. On the surface, the letter seems to lack much theological depth. But a more careful analysis reveals the inseparable tie between our relationship with God and with others: because God has embraced his enemies as family in Christ, so now we are to adopt a new, radical approach to our relationships.

For many, when we think about being a Christian, there is a sense in which we feel the need to do *great* things for a *great* God. If you have attended Christian conferences, you have probably heard the speaker say something along the lines of, "Who wants to win this continent for the Lord? Who here will become the next Billy Graham?" and so forth. In the Bible, there are some people, like Jeremiah and the apostle Paul, who were called to do extraordinary things. But what's interesting is that, on the whole, people in the Bible were called to live somewhat ordinary lives.[1] The Letter to Philemon is yet another reminder of this.

Philemon is an entire letter dedicated to making the point that Christians must embrace people, especially other Christians, whom they don't particularly like. Such people are annoying, smell,

---

1. One of the best treatments of this thesis is by Michael Horton, who states that "we must turn from the frantic search for 'something more' to 'something more sustainable.' We need to stop adding something more of ourselves to the gospel . . . We need to be content with his ordinary means of grace, that, over time, yield a harvest of plenty for everyone to enjoy" (*Ordinary*, 126).

talk too much, or talk too little. These are the people from whom we keep a safe distance and who seem to offer little, if anything at all, that would enhance our lives. It's noteworthy that God would set apart an entire letter just to deal with this ordinary topic of connecting with people that we don't want to connect with. Why? The reason seems straightforward. Before trying to accomplish wonderful things for God, God wants us to first change something far more basic—the way we engage people.

I think regularly about this point of prioritizing reconciliation for two reasons. First, human tendency is to remake God and Christianity in our own image. That is, we decide what's really important even if God has told us otherwise. For example, in Matthew 5:21–24 Jesus says:

> You have heard that it was said to those of old, "You shall not murder; and whoever murders will be liable to judgment." But I say to you that everyone who is angry with his brother will be liable to judgment; whoever insults his brother will be liable to the council; and whoever says, "You fool!" will be liable to the hell of fire. So if you are offering your gift at the altar and there remember that your brother has something against you, leave your gift there before the altar and go. First be reconciled to your brother, and then come and offer your gift.

This is an extraordinary command—to first be reconciled to your brother and then come and worship. Almost any Christian would agree that worship takes precedence over anything. In his book *Let the Nations Be Glad!*, John Piper makes the observation that someday the work of missions will cease but worship will flow into eternity.[2] Similarly, Luke ends his Gospel with the disciples meeting regularly to worship: "And they worshiped him and returned to Jerusalem with great joy, and were continually in the

2. Piper, *Let the Nations Be Glad!*, 35: "Missions is not the ultimate goal of the church. Worship is. Missions exist because worship doesn't. Worship is ultimate, not missions, because God is ultimate, not man. When this age is over, and the countless millions of the redeemed fall on their faces before the throne of God, missions will be no more. It is a temporary necessity. But worship abides forever."

temple blessing God" (Luke 24:52–53). Instead of engaging in a frenzy of evangelism, they worship the resurrected Jesus and thank God for the blessing of salvation.[3] So, none can deny the importance—the priority—of worship in the life of believers. Yet, even with this reality, Jesus has the audacity to hit the pause button on worship and reorient his disciples toward the restoration of relationships. Jesus doesn't even care if a believer is fine with the current state of affairs—rather, if "*your brother* has something against you," you must go and initiate reconciliation.

Given the priority that Jesus places on restored relationships, it is striking that many believers live with either a low view of reconciliation or an indifference toward it. A refusal to pursue reconciliation has become an "acceptable sin."[4] Somehow we have convinced ourselves and others to believe that God is OK with a pervasive state of broken relationships, all the more if we are busying ourselves with good works. However, if we take a step back, a refusal to seriously consider this reconciliation mandate is analogous to approaching the throne of grace and saying to our king, "I know you've asked me for *this*, but I've brought you *that* instead." The prophet's words are most fitting here: "Behold, to obey is better than sacrifice" (1 Sam 15:22).

Second, similar to the first reason for thinking about reconciliation, what I have experienced over the years among church leaders is a blatant refusal to take steps toward reconciliation. This is ironic and consequential given their position. On the one hand, they will regularly teach on the importance of reconciliation. They'll exhort members of their congregation to pursue peace before they partake in the family meal of communion. They'll mediate forgiveness between members. But when conflicts arise that concern them directly, they'll refuse to initiate or accept overtures toward restored relationships. Not only is this hypocritical but it is also noticeable. Their members are not oblivious and—as is the case with children and parents—many members learn just

---

3. See my comments in *A New King*, 67–69.

4. This general idea of "acceptable sins" is teased out in Jerry Bridges, *Respectable Sins*.

as much, if not more, from the example of their leaders. The need to recover this lost mandate to "go" and "be reconciled to your brother, and then come and offer your gift" needs to be recovered, especially among those who have been called to lead others.

Years ago I wrote a book entitled *True Faith*. It's a brief reflection on Paul's Letter to Titus. I had written my dissertation on it, and so I had the opportunity to reflect on its main message—that saving faith must be accompanied by good works in hope of eternal life.[5] The apostle Paul makes abundantly clear that a person is saved by faith, not by works (Titus 3:5). Yet the entire letter is preoccupied with the necessity of good works that demonstrate true faith. Paul makes the provocative statement that there are many who "profess to know God, but they deny him by their works" (Titus 1:16), or to be specific, by their lack of good works. Along these lines, I wonder if a disregard to prioritize what God prioritizes should give us reason to pause and think deeply about the veracity of our faith. I wonder if someday when we stand before Jesus and say, "Lord, did I not do *that* for you?" he will say, "But did you do *this* for me—did you heed my mandate to seek reconciliation?"

My main objective in this book is to help recover this lost mandate. I also address the related disciplines of mediation and winsome speech. All in all, my hope is to persuade sincere believers that reconciliation needs to play a pivotal role in their spirituality and must be done with wisdom and patience. Whether this is racial reconciliation, reconciliation between fellow members, or reconciliation between family and friends, we simply cannot continue to disregard this basic mandate in the name of ministry or because of general busyness. There are already excellent books—I have in mind especially Ken Sande's *The Peacemaker*—that detail more of the mechanics.[6] While I touch on some practical steps toward reconciliation, my goal is plain and simple: to exhort all who profess to follow Jesus to renew their commitment to pursue reconciliation.

---

5. See my comments in *True Faith*, 3–4, 25, 31, 37–39.

6. A few other good resources include: Love, *Peace Catalysts*; Katongole and Rice, *Reconciling All Things*; Van Yperen, *Making Peace*.

Also, I adopt an indirect approach to the subject in order to honor the style of the letter itself. Rather than addressing head-on the conflict between Philemon and Onesimus, Paul adopts a more circuitous path, reflecting on his imprisoned state, his personal relationship with Philemon and Onesimus, and the mysterious hand of God possibly at work. Similarly, this book is more of an extended meditation on reconciliation, mediation, and winsome persuasion instead of a systematic analysis of these topics. I trust the Spirit will take these reflections and draw believers to the point of appreciating the restored priority that reconciliation should play in their lives. Perhaps, then, we will all consider taking one or two steps toward creating cultures of peacemaking.

In closing, we should remember the important and inseparable connection between reconciliation and mission (the work of evangelism). Jesus said, "By this all people will know that you are my disciples, if you have love for one another" (John 13:35). How ordinary! The problem is that we live in the "age of the extraordinary." Everything we do must be exceptional and radical—including our evangelistic efforts. We must hold spectacular conferences that yield a conversion rate. We must thoroughly equip ourselves to possess the knowledge and wit of Tim Keller or Ravi Zacharias. We must offer fun and fancy student programs that can compete with Disney. To be clear, none of these is inherently "wrong." But perhaps our preoccupation with the extraordinary—even in our evangelism—contributes not only to our neglect of the ordinary call to pursue peace and reconciliation among believers, but also to our inability to trust that God will use such ordinary obedience to draw many to Christ. Perhaps the most radical thing we can do now is to pause from the extraordinary and commit ourselves anew to the ordinary work of making peace. I am confident that there will be extraordinary evangelical results from a deep commitment to fulfill this lost mandate to go and be reconciled.

1

Identity

Philemon 1–3, 23–25[1]

THIS CHAPTER ORIENTS US to the practice of Christian reconciliation by exploring the topic of identity. This might surprise some:
why speak on identity when the subject of the book is reconciliation? The apostle Paul rightly discerns that there are some more
basic matters we need to address first—in this case, the topic of
identity. As such, Paul explores the topic from three angles: identity and divinity, identity and community, and identity and mercy.
As we reflect on these points, it should become clear how identity
and reconciliation relate to each other.

---

1. The selection of these "bookend" verses is not arbitrary—there is a
linguistic and literary basis. Most likely, Philemon follows a chiastic arrangement, that is, a literary structure that follows the A-B-C-C'-B'-A' pattern. In
this arrangement, verses 1–3 and 23–25 form the A and A' units, respectively.
The parallelism between these two units is established through the unique occurrences of "prisoner" (1, 23), "fellow worker" (1, 24), and "grace" from "the
Lord Jesus Christ" (3, 25). For more details on this chiastic structure, see Heil,
"Chiastic Structure," 178–86.

Identity and Divinity

The letter begins with Paul identifying himself as "a prisoner for Christ Jesus" (v. 1a). In this brief identification, Paul gives some insight into how any believer should address the basic question "Who am I?" Notice the parts and order:

1. name—"Paul"

2. circumstance—"a prisoner"

3. perspective—"for Christ Jesus"

The first part is straightforward: "Paul, Jill, Fred." Everyone has a name. The second focuses on Paul's situation. This is worth highlighting. Our circumstances matter because we are physical creatures and are thus impacted by our physical circumstances.[2] The Bible doesn't minimize the fact that part of your identity is rooted in your circumstances. Paul is a "prisoner." You are a comedian. I am married with children. Biblical spirituality encourages us to have a sober appreciation for the material.[3]

---

2. From beginning to end—creation to resurrection—the Bible grounds humanity in physical conditions. Professor Stephen D. Snobelen elaborates: "Like vegetation and animals, Adam is made of the earth" ("Biblical View of Nature," 346). Snobelen goes on to point out that "[t]he teaching of the bodily resurrection provides yet another biblical affirmation of the essential goodness of the physical world" (ibid.).

3. Christian Counseling & Education Foundation (CCEF) advocates the consideration of a person's circumstances before performing a heart analysis. Counselor Robert W. Kellemen observes: "While we must focus here [on the comprehensive capacities of the heart], we can't ignore the relationship between the heart and two central arenas of influence: the body (we are embodied beings) and our social environment (we are embedded beings)" (*Gospel-Centered Counseling*, 111). He gives this example: "While the Bible steers us away from genetic determinism (that biology is the primary cause of our behavior), it does recognize that what happens in the body can affect us spiritually (e.g., Job 2:4–6)" (ibid., 112).

In my experience with pastoral counseling, sometimes people "need" a change in circumstance—even if this is temporary—in order to have the rest and clarity to later perform a deeper analysis involving the heart and motives. For instance, sometimes a person is so exhausted from constant work and a failure to sabbath that the best thing he or she can do is take a vacation.

Paul, however, goes one step further. He indicates that while circumstances play a role in identity formation, they should not play the ultimate role (which they often do). Instead, there should be something deeper, a God-oriented perspective that enables you to interpret and even transcend the immediate circumstance.[4] Paul doesn't just say that he's a "prisoner." He says he is "a prisoner for Christ Jesus."[5] By doing so, he is asserting that he is not just a prisoner, which would stir feelings of failure, injustice, and defeat. He is also—and more—one who is suffering for the sake of Christ and the gospel. Because he has this perspective, he can remain hopeful in an otherwise disheartening and difficult situation.

The same goes for us. Our identity doesn't have to depend on our circumstance. Instead, it can rest on something greater, something deeper, something unchanging. That something is our union with Christ Jesus.

Stability and Worth

The question of identity is one of the most basic human preoccupations. We see it all over. Just read any memoir and you'll see how it always comes back to the question "Who am I?" In the face of what feels like constantly changing circumstances, we want a clear and stable sense of self.

Sometimes married couples can best address conflict by taking a break from communicating. A right appreciation for the physical can do wonders for the spiritual.

4. Professor of Theology Don Schweitzer comments: "Human identity is partly a matter of one's genetic and cultural heritage, time and place of birth, social location, and so forth. But it is also a matter of the beliefs and values one becomes committed to" (*Jesus Christ for Contemporary Life*, 200). Ibid., 188: "A Christian's ultimate identity is determined by Jesus Christ, not by themselves. It is Jesus who is the Christ and not the church."

5. Two interpretations here are possible and are not necessarily exclusive. The first is that Paul is a prisoner *for* the sake of Christ and the gospel. That is, his obedience to Christ's call to preach the gospel to the Gentiles is why he is imprisoned. The second is that Paul is a prisoner *of* Christ Jesus (which is a literal translation of the Greek) in the sense that, ultimately, he is where he is because of the sovereignty of God. Paul is not at the mercy of Caesar but under the gracious rule of a sovereign God—even if that entails imprisonment.

We need at least two things to achieve this.[6] The first is a clear sense of *self*, one that is constant when life is not. In his book *Making Sense of God*, Timothy Keller summarizes:

> You live in many spheres at once. You are a family member at home, a colleague at work, a friend, and sometimes you are alone in solitude. To have an identity is to have something sustained that is true of you in every setting. Otherwise there would be no "you." There would be only masks for every occasion but no actual face behind them.[7]

Paul is in prison. At one point he was an elite Pharisee. Sometimes he had plenty to eat, sometimes very little. So who is he? He is a person united to Christ, which makes him a fully forgiven and adopted child of God destined for glory. Despite whatever might come his way, his identity is fixed because it is rooted in God, who doesn't change like shifting shadows.

The second ingredient for a strong identity is a sense of *worth*. "Self-knowledge is one thing, but self-regard is another. It is one thing to know what you are like; it's another thing to appreciate it."[8] Some people think very highly of themselves when they really shouldn't (e.g., the abusive spouse). Others don't think very highly of themselves and, to be frank, this is fitting. They've lived cruel and selfish lives, hating and being hated. And some have an accurate sense of self but an inconsistent self-regard. Christians, for instance, know that they're forgiven and righteous in Christ and destined for glory. Yet, their self-regard doesn't reflect these realities.

The gospel asserts that only in Christ can a person have a "positive" self-regard that is based on reality and doesn't depend on circumstances. Consider the alternative. If you base your identity on your situation, two things will happen. First, your sense of worth will constantly fluctuate. When life goes well, you feel great about yourself and great about life. But when life doesn't go well, you feel defeated and perhaps even worthless. Life, in other words,

---

6. Keller, *Making Sense of God*, 118.

7. Ibid.

8. Ibid.

begins to feel like an unending rollercoaster ride. In stark contrast, those in Christ experience a constant sense that all will be well because their identity is rooted in the unchanging One.

Second, if circumstances instead of Christ become the basis of self-worth, you will inevitably become competitive. This is because you need to improve your circumstances in order to feel equal, if not superior, to others. And this often requires pulling others down in order to elevate yourself. Sure, you may not be as obviously competitive as the contestants on *The Bachelor*. But in your heart you'll experience a constant mix of anger, elation, frustration, and competition.

In Christ, life becomes more stable because our identity rests in the unchanging love of Christ Jesus. In him we are confident that nothing can separate us from God's love. Also, because we believe that all we are and need is found in him, there is a sense of self-forgetfulness and a loss of a competitive mindset.[9] Our eyes are still very much fixed on others, but for a different reason. We're now free to think first and foremost about helping others instead of beating them.[10] And all this is possible without losing sight of reality. If anything, our relationship with Christ enables us to see reality more clearly. After all, to view life purely from a physical perspective is to fail to see life as it really is.[11]

---

9. See Keller, *Freedom of Self-Forgetfulness*, who articulates how Christian self-forgetfulness is a matter of identity: "It is very hard to get through a whole day without feeling snubbed or ignored or feeling stupid or getting down on ourselves. That is because there is something wrong with my ego. There is something wrong with my identity . . . it is always drawing attention to itself" (16–17).

10. Citing C. S. Lewis, Keller says it like this: "The thing we would remember from meeting a truly gospel-humble person is how much they seemed to be totally interested in us. Because the essence of gospel-humility is not thinking more of myself or thinking less of myself, it is thinking of myself less" (ibid., 32).

11. See, e.g., 1 Kings 2:1–14. Here, Elijah prays for Elisha, his apprentice, asking God to help him to gain a perspective that goes beyond his physical perception.

A Basic Test

How do you know whether you're rooting your identity in Christ or circumstances? Perhaps, the best way to know—unfortunately—is to see what you're like when life doesn't work out.

Several years ago, one of my seminary students asked me to pray for him. He had received an email from his employer. The company was downsizing. Everyone was on the chopping block. He became very anxious and couldn't sleep for about a month. After the ordeal passed, he reflected on this time and shared: "I began to realize that in spite of all my spiritual accomplishments—I'm a seminary student, a pastor in training, and an elder at my church—I still base my identity and security on things other than Jesus. I would have never thought this about myself had I not gone through this trial."

More positively, I recall when a couple shared that they had just received word that their child was diagnosed with down syndrome. As the pregnancy continued, they found out that their child might not survive. What struck me was the way in which they handled themselves with so much grace and hope. Sure, they were sad and didn't try to hide their sadness. But they weren't defeated—they wept like those with hope. Their perspective on the situation was simple: "God loves us the same now as ever. Even now God is working good."[12]

When life is going to well, it's easy to believe, "My identity is in Jesus." But God will often use tough circumstances to make us more self-aware. Trials will reveal how we're finding our meaning and security in things outside of Christ (or not). This doesn't explain all suffering in life and this isn't the only benefit of suffering. But it is an important benefit we can grow to appreciate when faced with "imprisonment."

How does all this relate to reconciliation? Two common obstacles to reconciliation are admitting failure and dealing with

---

12. The topic of suffering is real and difficult. Yet, the message of the cross is a vivid reminder that God can work good in the face of deep evil. See my comments in *A New King*, 7–15.

difficult people. In the first instance, we don't want to acknowledge that we have failed because doing so forces us to look in the mirror and admit that we're not as good and kind as we think. In the second instance, we simply don't want to deal with sensitive people who suffer from excessive egos. But an identity in Christ liberates us from both and moves us toward reconciliation. In Christ, we have learned to confess our sins; thus, confessing our shortcomings to others shouldn't feel all that foreign. Similarly, in Christ, we have received grace upon grace; thus, we have supernatural power (literally) to extend patience and kindness even to the most difficult people. In short, our divine identity as fully forgiven sinners empowers us to become agents of reconciliation.

Identity and Community[13]

After rooting his identity in Christ, Paul speaks of his relationship with other believers: "To Philemon our beloved *fellow* worker . . . and [to] Archippus our *fellow* soldier" (vv. 1b–2a); "Epaphras, my *fellow* prisoner in Christ Jesus, sends greetings to you, and so do Mark, Aristarchus, Demas, and Luke, my *fellow* workers" (vv. 23–24). Paul's identity is rooted not just in Christ but also in the community of believers. As the repeated use of "fellow" indicates, the church consists of those who enjoy a common fellowship in Christ.

Notice how verse 2 ends: "the church in your house." We often mistake the building where the church meets as the church. My son noted my own carelessness. On one Sunday, his little brother asked, "Where are we going?" I responded, "We're going to church." My first son interjected: "No, *we're* the church—we're going to meet with other Christians at the building." The church comprises those who are already one in Christ. Christian community is not something we're trying to build, especially through a building. Christian community is something that already exists because of Christ and his gospel.

---

13. This is so important that we develop it further in the next chapter.

This point is important to highlight because we tend to allow other things to shape our relationships. The first is preference—comfort and chemistry. The second is utility—"What does this person offer me?" Both are natural tendencies and understandable. But followers of Christ are called to be deliberate about all facets of life, especially when it comes to community.

Modernity has changed people's view of community. In the past, identity was tied to community (probably excessively so). Pastor Duane Larson writes:

> It used to be the case, and not so long ago, that a person would know who she or he was and what she or he would do vocationally from a very early age. It was expected or simply understood that Jim would grow up to be a farmer or a salesperson or a pastor because dad and grandad and great-granddad had done likewise.[14]

We see an example of this in the Academy Award winning movie *Forrest Gump*.[15] Lieutenant Dan "was from a long, great military tradition. Somebody in his family had fought *and died* in every single American war." But after Forrest saves him from dying in the Vietnam War, Lieutenant Dan angrily says to Forrest: "I *should have died* out there with my men, but now, I'm nothing . . . I was Lieutenant Dan Taylor." This approach to identity was more prevalent before modernity.[16]

But things have changed. Now identity is less about connecting with community and tradition. It's about being true to yourself. Keller says:

> In Western cultures the new heroic narrative is *self-assertion*. You are your individual dreams and desires, and your self-worth depends on the dignity you bestow on yourself, because you have asserted your dreams and

14. Larson, "Life Together," 15–16.

15. Screenplay for *Forrest Gump* by Eric Roth.

16. Notably, in a scene near the end of the movie where Lt. Dan makes peace with God, he says to Forrest, "I never thanked you for saving my life." It's in this moment that he begins to experience a new identity—one that is no longer connected to lineage but to God.

desires regardless of the opposition you may have had from the community.[17]

Consider the recent installment of the Star Wars saga *The Last Jedi*. The movie asserts that you don't have to know your past to forge an identity into the future.[18] You are whoever you choose to be. This is Kevin Hart's thesis in his hilarious memoir *I Can't Make This Up*:

> Your life today is the sum total of your choices. So if you're not happy with it, look back at your choices and start making different ones. Even if you are struck by lightning and injured, you made choices that led you to that spot at a particular time—and you get to choose how you feel about it afterward.[19]

I'm not suggesting that everything about this modern change is bad. Formerly, the poor stayed poor and the rich became richer because of the pervasive maxim "know your place."[20] The modern view of identity encourages individuals to break through preset—and often unfair—limits. There is something very helpful and good to this perspective.[21] In fact, the gospel itself gives us a new story to live by.

Still, this modern approach to identity has created many problems. Among other things, it has weakened community. Philosopher Charles Taylor asserts that this approach minimizes community to being "purely instrumental in their significance."[22]

---

17. Keller, *Making Sense of God*, 120.

18. The character Kylo Ren declares: "Let the past die. Kill it, if you have to. That's the only way to become what you are meant to be." Screenplay for *Star Wars: The Last Jedi* by Rian Johnson.

19. Hart with Strauss, *I Can't Make This Up*, 19.

20. See Keller, *Making Sense of God*, 121.

21. Consider the examples of Jeff Bezos and Steve Jobs. Biographer Ann Byers says of Bezos: "Most of the things Jeff did, he did a little differently than everyone else . . . Jeff's 'different-ness' helped him overcome what would have been difficult hurdles to anyone less determined" (*Jeff Bezos*, 18–19). As for Jobs, he harnessed his painful past of being "given up at birth" to become one of the greatest technological revolutionaries of all time (Isaacson, *Steve Jobs*, 4).

22. Taylor, *Ethics of Authenticity*, 43.

Community is not where we find identity; it's where we find utility. The thought is, "If this community helps me to advance my dreams, I stick with it. If it doesn't, I move on." Consumerism is not limited to what we purchase on Amazon. It also influences our approach to relationships, elevating our preferences and needs above anything else.

Many Christians approach church in this way. When they go to church, their main question isn't, "What's the leadership like?" or, "Is the gospel preached every week?" or, "Is the community committed to justice and mercy?" Instead personal desires—important but not central—take center stage. "Are there people like me?" "Can I meet a potential spouse?" "Do I like the music?"[23] In most cases, these consumeristic bonds are weak, lasting only insofar as the community is performing its function.

This "culture of utility" represents the exact opposite of the mindset promoted by the Bible. The biblical perspective on community is that diverse individuals are brought together by one Lord and one gospel. A Christian, then, does not pursue relationships on the basis of potential or conditional usefulness. Rather, a Christian seeks to deepen relationships that Christ has already made through himself. New Testament scholar Douglas J. Moo writes:

> This short private letter stands . . . as an important reminder of the communitarian aspect of Christianity that many of us, in our individualist cultures, are so prone to forget. In Christ we belong to one another; we enjoy each other's company and support; and we are obliged to support, to the point of sacrificing our own time, interest, and money, our brothers and sisters.[24]

23. Larson, "Life Together," 15: "When I 'shop' for a church, I join finally that congregation which most suits my preferences of class, or lifestyle, or worship style, or politics, and so on. Again, this activity of differentiation is not a negative one necessarily. But notice the omissions from the examples of criteria. When I 'church shop,' I do not ask what I can do for the congregation and its mission. I do not ask how it needs me. I am a church shopper when I lay claim to the congregation instead of allowing the congregation to lay claim to me. As the individual—as an individualist—I, the church shopper, and I only set the terms."

24. Moo, *Letters*, 378.

Each year during the holiday season people of every background adopt this biblical approach to community with their in-laws. Some love their in-laws, some don't. But when it comes to Thanksgiving and other familial obligations, the question is not, "Do I like them?" or, "Are they easy to get along with?" The more basic question is, "Like it or not they're my family, and we're bound by something beyond personal preferences. Therefore, what do I need to do to make it work?" That's the biblical approach. Community is not a matter of chemistry, preference, or convenience. It's about pursuing a reality that is already true in Christ. Maturing as a believer requires adopting the mindset of "making this work." It's not by accident that when Paul speaks of love in the well-known 1 Corinthians 13 passage, he says that love is first and foremost long-suffering ("patient").

Professor A. J. Swoboda comments:

> [A]ll of us at some level attempt to create a community that makes sense. But I have to think that when it doesn't make sense and you have all of these weird people, then maybe the one thing that's gathering us is not politics, it's not whether we like this preacher or that church, or whether we listen to this podcast or another, but that the thing that brings us together is a celebration of the death of Christ.[25]

In this sense, Christian relationships will feel very unnatural because God is drawing to himself people from every tribe, tongue, and nation. God is the true pluralist—the only really open-minded person—who is bringing together people who would otherwise never be in the same room. Growing in maturity means accepting and pursuing relationships that don't "feel right."

As an aside, this is why small group ministries are good and perhaps even necessary. Consider how all the names Paul mentions are from Jewish *and* Gentile backgrounds. In other words, his "partners" and "soldiers" for the gospel do not come from the same ethnic group. This is important to emphasize because many Christians today believe that they don't really need to join a small

25. Swoboda, "The Cross Creates a Paradox."

group. They reason that they already have Christian community and accountability: "It's not like I'm a solo believer doing life by myself. I have Christian friends." But these friends tend to be people of similar background. They all feel, think, talk, and act alike. Small groups, however, are great because they offer the opportunity to show love toward people who are so different from us.[26]

This relationship between identity and community plays an important role in understanding the Bible's teaching on reconciliation. The point is straightforward: be reconciled to one another because all believers are your family in Christ. As we noted, modern individualism has weakened the force of this familial framework. Today, the modern impulse is so strong that more than a few are willing to cut ties easily even with family. The Bible, however, assumes a high view of family; if we adopt this view, the basic relationship between identity, community, and reconciliation becomes self-evident: be reconciled because you're family. As we'll see in this letter, Paul basically says, "Philemon, be reconciled with Onesimus because he's your brother in the Lord."

Identity and Mercy

All this sounds wonderful, but how do we move toward reconciliation, especially with those whom we dislike? How do you love the recalcitrant and self-righteous? Paul provides some insight in the opening and concluding verses.

Paul begins this letter differently from many of his other letters. His usual introduction is "Paul, an *apostle* of Christ Jesus."[27] The term "apostle" signals authority and power.[28] But here he says,

26. Ibid.: "People who study people [sociologists] have long been telling us that people find affinity with people that they are sort of similar to—what we call affinity: they find community with others that they agree with . . . But [with] Jesus, you almost kind of wonder. If he was here, he would look at you and say, 'Sociologists, they're wrong!' because Jesus intentionally created communities of people who would otherwise completely hate each other."

27. See 2 Cor 1:1; Gal 1:1; Eph 1:1; Col 1:1; 1 Tim 1:1; 2 Tim 1:1. Similarly, Rom 1:1; 1 Cor 1:1; Titus 1:1.

28. As New Testament scholar Richard B. Gaffin Jr. notes, "an apostle of

"Paul, a *prisoner* for Christ Jesus."[29] This deviation from his usual introduction is intentional. With each word he wants to facilitate reconciliation between Philemon and Onesimus.

Philemon is a reputable man; he's powerful and wealthy enough to host the church in his home. Onesimus is a slave, a nobody; in short, the opposite of Philemon. No one knows exactly what Onesimus did, but it was bad enough that he felt like he had to run away.[30] At this point, knowing that his master Philemon esteems the apostle, Onesimus finds Paul and asks him to intercede on his behalf. During their time together, Onesimus comes to faith and is sent back to be reconciled to Philemon—with Paul serving as the mediator.

The problem is that Philemon wants no part in this. The reason is not entirely clear. Perhaps there is an element of socio-economic discrimination. The more likely reason is simply that Onesimus has wounded Philemon deeply. Thus, Philemon can't help but reject Onesimus. So what does Paul do? In this given situation, Philemon is the stronger of the two. He has more power, more prestige, more resources. Of course, by "nature"—status, etc.—Paul is more like Philemon than Onesimus. But he "incarnates" and identifies with

---

Christ is someone uniquely authorized by the exalted Christ to speak authoritatively for him. Regarding this authority, the apostle is as Christ himself" (*By Faith*, 14–15).

29. James D. G. Dunn comments: "Elsewhere, from Galatians on, it was Paul's almost unvarying practice to 'pull rank' by stressing his apostleship" (*Epistles*, 310).

30. Barth and Blanke, *Letter to Philemon*, 141: "That Onesimus had run away from his master is unanimously presupposed by practically all readers and scholarly expositors of PHM. Recent attempts to deny that Onesimus had broken law and order are not (yet?) persuasive." As to what exactly Onesimus did and why he felt like he had to leave, several suggestions have been put forward, but there is no consensus. Scholar Ben Witherington offers this observation: "Paul writes as if Onesimus owes Philemon something important. At the very least he owed him the time of service he has been away from Colossae, but in addition he owed him himself; he was Philemon's property, not free to go off on his own without his master's permission. He may also have taken some money with him when he fled. The legal language of wrongdoing [in] Philemon (v. 18) seems to suggest a more serious situation than just a domestic dispute over something (e.g., that the slave has been indolent or useless)" (*Letters*, 28).

Onesimus by referring to himself as a "prisoner"—one without any rights, an outcast. Professor Alicia J. Batten observes: "Paul's explicit reference to imprisonment . . . has rhetorical power, for it underlines Paul's solidarity with the slave Onesimus . . ."[31] In this way, Paul models the principle of identification.

Only the gospel makes identification with outcasts, foreigners, and even enemies possible. The gospel invites everyone to take a look in the mirror in order to see that we're not as different from our transgressors as we think. Jonathan Edwards expressed this well:

> *Resolved*, To act, in all respects, both speaking and doing, as if nobody had been so vile as I, and as if I had committed the same sins, or had the same infirmities or failings, as others; and that I will let the knowledge of their failings promote nothing but shame in myself, and prove only an occasion of my confessing my own sins and misery to God.[32]

When Paul describes himself as a "prisoner" in order to identify with Onesimus, he undoubtedly has in view Christ's becoming a prisoner (literally) to identify with—and to free—those who were imprisoned by the power of sin.[33] In his Letter to the Philippians, Paul declares that though Jesus was God, Christ became a servant in order to exalt those who were rebels (2:6–8). Those who have experienced such grace have a new disposition toward their enemies, an "unnatural" desire to identify with those whom they would have otherwise separated from.

Paul knows that, by the standards of this world, he and Onesimus have nothing in common. Paul is an apostle, Onesimus is a slave. Still, seeing Onesimus, Paul recalls his own weakness and

31. Batten, "Philemon," 236.

32. Edwards, *Works*, xx.

33. John MacArthur: "Paul's willingness to meet Onesimus's debt to restore his relationship with Philemon is a marvelous picture of Christ's work. Philemon, like God, had been wronged. Onesimus, like the sinner, stood in need of reconciliation. Paul offered to pay the price to bring about the reconciliation. That is the same role Jesus plays in the relationship between the sinner and God. Paul, like Christ, was willing to pay the price of reconciliation" (*Colossians & Philemon*, 224).

powerlessness in salvation, so much so that the Son of Man had to die in his place. Having experienced such kindness, Paul chooses to do likewise by identifying with Onesimus. Similarly, he chooses to intercede for the disenfranchised because the Son of God interceded on his behalf. In sum, it's the gospel that moves us from viewing our opponents as foreign entities and sinful specimens to extending the sort of mercy we have experienced in Christ.

Paul himself models what it means to show grace. At the close of the letter, Paul mentions "Mark" (v. 24). Mark had joined Paul and Barnabas on their first missionary journey (Acts 12:25) but left them when ministry became difficult (Acts 13:13). Later when Mark tried to rejoin Paul on his second missionary journey, Paul refused him (Acts 15:37–38). However, in Paul's later letters (Phlm, 2 Tim), we see that the two had been reconciled and that Mark had become one of Paul's most loyal and useful companions.

How was this reconciliation possible? Paul, a failure who had received mercy from Christ, was now able to show mercy to another failure. Eventually, Paul himself was able to see that he and Mark were not all that different. Paul, after all, had tried to destroy the church. But Jesus responded to his persecution by making him a champion of the gospel. Having received such mercy, how could he see himself as better than Mark? In Paul, we see that an identity rooted in mercy makes gospel-community and reconciliation possible. This is his challenge to Philemon. It's his challenge to us.

Who is your Onesimus? When you see this person, is it impossible to identify with his or her shortcomings? The gospel declares that "all have sinned and fall short of the glory of God" (Rom 3:23). Obviously, we have not all sinned in the same way or to the same degree. But in the end, "None is righteous, no, not one" (Rom 3:10). Yet, Christ drew near to us, identified with us to the point of dying in our place, so that we might be reconciled to God. We who have received such mercy should then be the most merciful people;[34] and such mercy should take the form of identifying

---

34. Sande writes similarly: "Christians are the most forgiven people in the world. Therefore, we should be the most forgiving people in the world" (*Peacemaker*, 204).

with our opponents. Left to ourselves, this is impossible. Literally. But through the gospel, we can become agents of reconciliation by identifying with our enemies as fellow sinners in need of grace.

Summary

Identity, community, and mercy represent basic building blocks for fostering a culture of reconciliation. Above anything else, we belong to Christ, our Lord and Savior. We are not free to live however we please. Rather, we live under his lordship and for his glory. Moreover, in Christ we have received the Spirit of adoption and now belong to the fellowship of the saints: a union with Christ and participation in his family go hand-in-hand. It cannot be otherwise. I am just as much a son or daughter of God as I am a brother or sister to other believers. This reality helps us to see why reconciliation is not an option but a mandate: as God has reconciled himself to us in Christ, so too we must be reconciled to one another. Thanks be to God that such power and perspective are made available to us through the gospel. We can identify with sinners because we have One who identified with us in order to bring us into the perfect fellowship of the Father, Son, and Holy Spirit.[35]

35. In his comments on the term "fellowship," Moo brings together well all the themes we have covered: "The word [fellowship] captures a central concern of the letter: to highlight the reality of the close and intimate 'fellowship' that Christians enjoy with one another as a fundamental basis for the way we perceive ourselves and for the way that we are to respond to specific situations . . . When people believe in Christ, they become identified with one another in an intimate association and incur both the benefits and responsibilities of that communion" (*Letters*, 392).

2

Community

Philemon 4–7

IN THE LAST CHAPTER, we considered the basic elements of identity, community, and mercy as they relate to reconciliation. We now consider the topic of community in more detail. Again, Paul does not yet directly address the subject of reconciliation. He is still laying the groundwork for helping Philemon and all believers understand the necessity and priority of reconciliation in the Christian life. Also, he is modeling wise communication in tense situations: sometimes, it is more effective to take a more circuitous path. In this chapter, we consider the tie between faith and community, our need for community, and our responsibility toward community.

Faith and Community

After Paul's introduction comes his characteristic thanksgiving-prayer (v. 4). He thanks God for Philemon: "I hear of your love and of the faith that you have toward the Lord Jesus and for all the saints" (v. 5). Here, Paul brings together the horizontal and the vertical—our love toward God's people and our faith in the Lord Jesus Christ.[1] He is reiterating a basic point in the Bible, namely

1. There is an obvious chiastic arrangement here:

that you cannot separate your relationship with God and your relationship with his family. They must always be held together.

Faith in the Lord Jesus

Let's first consider faith in the Lord Jesus. The reason why we want to emphasize this basic part of Christianity is because human tendency is to put faith in the self, to seek self-justification. Think about how you respond to criticism. If a person points out a weakness, you almost immediately try to justify yourself.

This tendency never goes away. Even Christians revert back to self-justification. For example, suppose before you were a believer, you were not generous; after conversion, you give away huge sums of money. This is wonderful! But what can happen is that you begin to believe that God is on your side because of your good works. This is why we always need to remind ourselves that we are saved by faith alone, not by our good works. That's why Paul begins his prayer by thanking God for "the *faith* that you have toward the Lord Jesus" (v. 5): Philemon trusts that God's favor rests upon him not because of his own good life but because of the perfect life that Jesus lived on his behalf.

Noteworthy is the preposition "*toward* the Lord Jesus." Some feel like their faith isn't very strong and therefore God couldn't possibly love and accept them. Maybe that is the case—maybe their faith isn't very strong. But the emphasis here is not on the strength of a person's faith but on the object of faith—in this case, Jesus Christ.

In Mark's Gospel, Jesus dialogues with the father of a possessed boy. The father says, "But if you can do anything, have compassion on us and help us" (9:22). Jesus responds, "'If you can'! All things are possible for the one who believes" (9:23). Then the father confesses, "I believe; help my unbelief!" (9:24). In other words, "I

A: your love
B: your faith
B': in the Lord Jesus
A': for all the saints

have faith in you, but it's not very strong. Would you bless me even so?" Ultimately the boy is healed—not because the father had great faith but because his weak faith was in a great Savior. Paul thanks God for Philemon because Philemon has put his imperfect faith (as we'll see) in a perfect Savior.

It is worth highlighting the kind of salvation Paul has in mind. Paul specifies "the *Lord* Jesus" to make the point that believing in Jesus for salvation goes hand-in-hand with submitting to him as Lord. This point is especially relevant to our discussion on reconciliation because it addresses the basic attitude that we see often in conflict, namely a refusal to make peace. This is understandable. If anything, we should admit that reconciling is hard work and, in many ways, unnatural. But the basic question for a believer is not so much about what I want to do but more so what my Lord demands. It's a wonderful thing that God doesn't require tremendous faith in order to be saved: weak sinners may enter. At the same time, as we mature, we must realize that our Savior is our Lord, the one who has made clear the priority his disciples should place on reconciliation.

Love for All the Saints

Many believe that salvation is by faith, not by works: "It's not my resume that matters—it's Jesus's resume." But how do we know we have really trusted in Jesus? Paul answers this by pointing to our relationship with other believers. He teaches that the fruit of true faith toward Jesus is love and devotion to God's people.

Spirituality in the West is very individualistic.[2] "Western salvation" can be depicted in this way: a person is hanging off a

2. New Testament professor William W. Klein observes: "A renewed emphasis on the corporate nature of God's plan strongly confronts the individualistic 'me and Jesus' view of salvation that permeates western culture. Any fair reading of Paul's plea to the Philippians to 'continue to work out your salvation' (Phil 2:12), will acknowledge its corporate intent. We truncate God's grand strategy when we focus almost exclusively on what 'God has done for me.' Salvation is found in the body of Christ, the church" (*New Chosen People*, 306). More briefly, Franciscan priest Albert Haase says: "Christianity has never

cliff. Jesus comes, reaches down, picks him up. *Voilà*, the person is saved and follows Jesus the rest of his days. A more accurate depiction, however, inserts a believer between that person and the Lord: in order to be saved, he must cling to the in-between believer with all his might. The reason why this a more accurate portrayal of salvation is because it highlights that you cannot hold on to Jesus without holding on to his people.[3] Saving faith and Christian fellowship are two sides of the same coin.

Paul, however, presses the point. He asserts that Christians must exhibit a non-discriminatory love—they must have love "for *all* the saints." (v. 5). Love for the body of Christ is not limited to those you find tolerable or pleasant. It's not given only to those of similar socio-economic background. The text speaks of love "for *all* the saints," not love "for *select* saints."

Such inclusive love finds its roots in the gospel. The gospel declares that all have sinned—Jew and Gentile—and that all can be saved—Jew and Gentile—if they believe in Christ. In 1 Timothy 2:3–5 the apostle Paul writes: "This is good, and it is pleasing in the sight of God our Savior, who desires all people to be saved and to come to the knowledge of the truth. For there is one God, and there is one mediator between God and men, the man Christ Jesus." Notice how these verses capture both the inclusive and exclusive qualities of the gospel: all can be saved by trust in Christ alone.[4]

Such "indiscriminate love" should create a people known for "indiscriminate love."

The call to love all the saints, however, doesn't mean that the world is ours to save.[5] Given we are finite beings, it's impossible

---

promoted an individualistic 'me and Jesus' spirituality. Such thinking is an anomaly and an aberration" (*Coming Home*, 25).

3. In C. S. Lewis's *The Lion, the Witch, and the Wardrobe*, there is a scene that illustrates this point. The Lion, Aslan, represents Jesus and says to the children: "'We have a long journey to go. You must ride on me.' And he crouched down and the children climbed onto his warm, golden back, and Susan sat first, holding on tightly to his mane and Lucy sat behind holding on tightly to Susan" (118).

4. For further discussion, see my comments in *1 Timothy, Vol. 1*, 151–61.

5. For a helpful treatment on this topic, see Wigg-Stevenson, *The World Is*

to love everyone. What's helpful is identifying our main spheres of influence and responsibility. My main spheres are my family and friends, my church, and my seminary. Seeking to love the people in these three groups is how I try to work out love "for all the saints."

Still, I would offer one word of caution about this approach. When my wife was pregnant with our firstborn son, I was attending a church comprised mostly of the same people—ethnically, socially, and economically. During this time a conviction weighed heavily on me. Jesus's final words to his disciples were, "Go therefore and make disciples of all nations" (Matt 28:19). John's vision of the future consists of "a great multitude . . . from every nation, from all tribes and peoples and languages . . ." (Rev 7:9). Yet, we were attending a church that was basically from one nation, tribe, people, and language. If the church were local, that could be a justification for attending. But it wasn't, and there were plenty of good churches much closer. What explanation would we give our son? How would we justify worshiping and doing life only with people who looked and talked like us? In this instance, my sphere of influence was basically my sphere of comfort and familiarity. My wife and I felt called to join a church where our spheres of influence might better reflect "*all* the saints."[6]

Not Ours To Save, who opens by saying: "because we know that the work is *God's* to bring about, we can labor without the anxiety of imagining that the welfare of history rises or ebbs on the tide of our own blood, sweat and tears" (22).

6. My purpose here is not to discount the legitimacy and even necessity of ethnic churches. Mark DeYmaz and Harry Li acknowledge that "the *homogeneous unit principle* . . . suggests that churches grow fastest when they're homogeneous—made up of people from the same ethnic, economic, and educational background. For the most part, the principle is true and can be used quite effectively to build a large church. In other words, target a specific group of people, appeal to their collective wants and wishes, and your church will grow" (*Ethnic Blends*, 21–22). However, as they point out: "The problem with the homogeneous unit principle is that despite the good intentions of those interested in rapidly reaching the world with the gospel (and consequently growing churches quickly), the principle has had the unintended effect of justifying the segregation of local congregations along ethnic and economic lines. The fact is, it has led us even further away from principles and practices that defined New Testament churches such as existed at Antioch and Ephesus—churches in which the love of God for *all* people was clearly on display

The Letter of 1 John summarizes Paul's point: "If anyone says, 'I love God,' and hates his brother, he is a liar; for he who does not love his brother whom he has seen cannot love God whom he has not seen" (4:20). As we continue to reflect on the topic of reconciliation, both Paul's words and John's words are impossible to ignore. What's striking and unsettling about these verses is their unambiguous quality: if you have genuine faith in the Lord Jesus, you will have love toward all the saints; or, if you lack love toward all the saints, you do not have true faith in Christ. In this sense, a stubborn refusal to love, forgive, and embrace all believers should give serious reason to pause and reflect over the authenticity of our faith.

Our Need for Community

In verse 6, Paul says, "and I pray that the sharing of your faith may become effective for the full knowledge of every good thing that is in us for the sake of Christ." The following paraphrase clarifies this convoluted statement: "I pray that your earnest participation in the fellowship of saints, a fellowship rooted in a common faith, will help you figure out every good thing God wants you to do—with and for other believers, all for the glory of Christ."[7] In short, only by living in God's community can we discern God's will for our lives. New Testament scholar James D. G. Dunn asserts: "The corporate character of the shared faith is central to the thought; Paul had no desire to promote the idea of religious faith as something private, that which a person enjoys alone and practices as a

---

. . ." (22). For further discussion on this topic, see Williams, *Church Diversity*, 47–53; Garces-Foley, *Crossing the Ethnic Divide*, 81–85; Webber, *Worship*, 254.

7. Wright, *Epistles*, 176–77: "Paul prays that the fact of this mutual participation will 'work powerfully' within Philemon to produce 'knowledge'. This 'knowledge' is not merely theoretical understanding but an integrated and operational grasp of 'every good thing', *i.e.* what God is doing in Christ and what he, Philemon, must do in consequence . . . If Philemon allows the principle of mutual participation (itself part of his faith in Christ) powerfully to inform his thinking and living, then the right results will follow."

separate individual."[8] If we are serious about pursuing the will of God, we must live in intimate fellowship with other believers.

The Bible teaches two types of revelation. On the one hand, there is "special" revelation, the few instances when God speaks directly to individuals. For example, God speaks to Adam, Noah, and Moses; Jesus speaks to his apostles. These instances of special revelation are limited to few persons in the history of redemption. Such individuals are spotlighted in biblical narratives, and many people end up naming their children after them. But when we compare the number of persons who have received such special revelation to the number of believers, "very few" is an understatement. Therefore, special revelation should not be understood as the ordinary means through which God reveals his will to his people.

On the other hand, there is "normal" revelation. It's when you figure out what God wants by listening to the preached Word of God and by living in biblical community. That's the way God "spoke" to the majority of people throughout the entire Bible. God rarely spoke directly to the Israelites in the Old Testament and to believers in the New Testament. Instead, the model in both the Old and New Testaments was that by hearing the public proclamation of the God's Word and by living in community, God's people could discern his will.

I highlight this because there's a model of spirituality today that leans toward "special" revelation. The problem, however, with this kind of well-intended piety is that it forgets the Bible's own witness, namely that special revelation was limited to select individuals in God's plan of salvation. The remaining 99.99 percent of God's people were expected to discern God's will through the canonized Word (i.e., the Bible) and Christian fellowship. I suspect that part of what contributes to this tendency is our preoccupation with the extraordinary. To discern God's will seems like such a lofty endeavor; therefore, we suppose that lofty means are necessary, something akin to extended times of meditation in hibernation from society or waiting on bended knee to hear God whisper into our hearts. I don't mean to suggest that personal retreats and

8. Dunn, *Epistles*, 319.

extended times of prayer are unhelpful or that special revelation can never happen. But the narrative and trajectory of the Bible suggest that such extraordinary means were exactly that—extraordinary—and that for the normal believer the ordinary means of the proclaimed Word and Christian fellowship are sufficient for knowing and doing the will of God.

In the Book of Judges the repeated refrain to illustrate the downward spiral of Israel is, "Everyone did what was right in his own eyes" (e.g., 17:6; 21:25). What we see in the book is a fragmentation of Israel, which leads to increasing folly and violence. Similarly, in the well-known parable of the two lost sons, more commonly referred to as "The Prodigal Son," Jesus couples folly with a breakdown in community (Luke 15:11–32). The younger son wastes his life in reckless living and the older son drowns in bitterness as each turns away from the father. In a sense, this parable is about the breakdown in family as both sons do what is right in their own eyes. The message is clear: wisdom for life and discerning God's will are found by living in gospel community.

Discerning Our Gifts for the Edification of the Saints

There are several related applications we can draw from this general principle of needing Christian community. The first is that Christian fellowship provides the proper arena for discerning our spiritual gifts. In Ephesians 2:10 the apostle Paul makes clear that God's gift of salvation should not lead to a passive and unproductive life. For "we are his workmanship, created in Christ Jesus for good works, which God prepared beforehand, that we should walk in them." This is amazing news: not only have we been saved, but we have been saved unto good works that God has equipped us to carry out. The question now is, "How do we discern our gifts and calling?"

In the 1980s and 90s, the answer was "Spiritual Inventory" tests. You would go down a list, check everything that applies to you, and then—*presto*—you would know how God has gifted you and what you're supposed to do with your life. The odd thing about these tests was that somehow everyone was gifted in exactly the ways he or she wanted. In other words, the concluding data often represented the projected and desired images of the participants. The other problem with this approach was that it assumed people are very self-aware.[9] These basic observations reflect the weakness in this inventory-individualistic approach.

A sounder approach has three aspects, all of which involve community. First, there is something to looking at inventory together. With other believers we should study the various "gift lists" included in the Bible (e.g., Rom 12:1–8; 1 Cor 12:4–11, 28), then study together what each gift means and how it contributes to the edification of the saints. Second, consider your past experiences, your affinities, and what seem to be your more "natural" abilities.[10] The variety of gifts listed in the Bible is wide enough to find some match with your experiences, passions, and skills. Third, put your gifts into practice. We shouldn't suppose that the conclusions drawn from the first two steps are infallible. The third stage of practicing our gifts in community involves trial-and-error. In the process we may discover through the honest and gentle feedback of community where we are most gifted and effective.

9. Professors of Psychology Timothy D. Wilson and Nancy Brekke point out: "People's lay beliefs determine the steps they take (or fail to take) to correct their judgments and thus are an important but neglected source of biased responses" ("Mental Contamination and Mental Correction," 117). Psychologist Peter Gray adds: "The problem is that introspection is a private technique, and science requires public technique. A public technique is one that produces data that can be observed by outsiders, not just by the individual user of the procedure" (*Psychology*, 10). Dr. Braj Kumar Mishra concludes: "Self-observed facts are unverifiable and cannot be checked by other observers. Hence, not dependable. Self-observation reports are likely to be misreported or not honestly reported. Hence, not much reliable and analysis may go wrong" (*Psychology*, 50).

10. I have become doubtful about "natural" abilities. Geoff Colvin's *Talent is Overrated* makes the argument that deliberate practice—not natural talent—is what fosters exceptional human performance. In a lecture, Colvin gives the example that a person's ability to memorize is dramatically enhanced by "putting in the hours" ("Talent is Overrated"). Case in point is Kobe Bryant. In a 2007 *Esquire* article, Mike Sager describes what Bryant did to get back on top after an injury: "To correct the flaw, Kobe went to the gym over the summer and made one hundred thousand shots. That's one hundred thousand *made*, not taken. He doesn't practice taking shots, he explains. He practices making them" ("Kobe Bryant").

This third approach of testing and trying in community gives us freedom and pleasure to discover gifts that we would not have discerned on our own. Over the years many seminary students and church members have come to me and expressed something along the lines of, "I was asked to give a talk," or, "I was asked to lead a small group." None had supposed he or she was gifted to do it, but the need was there and so an effort was given. The surprising fruit and positive feedback from other members helped them to realize their gift in teaching and leading. Such discernment was only possible by abiding in community.

It's fascinating that a culture obsessed with trying to discover the self by looking within has made little progress in self-knowledge. I'm not suggesting that we can't know anything about ourselves from some introspection. But the Bible teaches that a "full knowledge of every good thing that is in us" comes from *outside us*—it comes only when we become committed members to a church. Larson comments: "our personhood is not fully realized or achieved unless we realize and achieve it within a community of faith."[11]

Coming to Faith

The second related application is that Christian community plays a critical role in facilitating conversion. Suppose you have people coming to your church who do not yet confess Jesus as their Lord and Savior. They're figuring things out, reading books, and listening to podcasts. All that is great—but insufficient. At some point they need to join a church. This is because people learn just as much—if not more—from direct experience. Expecting mothers read a lot before giving birth. Yet, much of the "real" learning takes place through the actual experience of raising a newborn. Similarly, we learn what Christianity is about just as much—if not more—from engagement with believers.

I have seen this happen many times at our church. Several years ago, a young professional shared his testimony prior to his baptism. He said that he started coming to church through the

11. Larson, "Life Together," 16.

invitation of a coworker. Over the span of a year, he read books on theology and philosophy, listened to podcasts from people for and against Christianity, and researched specific questions he had. But in the end, it was through deep and regular fellowship with believers that things "clicked." As he witnessed Christians loving others inside and outside of the church, he began to understand God's love for us in Christ. Their sincerity, generosity, and thoughtfulness (he had previously suspected that believers were unthinking people) helped him to overcome what he had considered insurmountable hurdles to conversion.

We were not made to be cognitive processors who convert to Christianity through the input of a set of facts. Because we are body-and-soul creatures, it shouldn't surprise us that our coming to faith will be a body-and-soul experience. To be clear, preaching the Word of God is absolutely necessary. We mustn't entertain the thought, "Preach the gospel; use words when necessary."[12] At the same time, God knew that an experience of gospel community would play a critical role in gospel conversion.[13] So our need for Christian fellowship begins even before conversion.

Examining Mark's Gospel, Heather Zempel discusses the scene when four men carried their paralyzed friend to Jesus, dismantled the roof, and lowered their friend to meet Jesus (Mark 2:1–12). Because of their faith, Jesus forgave the man's sins. She concludes:

12. Keller explains the problem with this idea: "The popular saying 'Preach the gospel; use words if necessary' is helpful but also misleading. If the gospel were primarily about what we must do to be saved, it could be communicated as well by actions (to be imitated) as by words. But if the gospel is primarily about what God has done to save us, and how we can receive it through faith, it can *only* be expressed through words" (*Center Church*, 32).

13. It is noteworthy there isn't a whole lot written about evangelistic programs in the New Testament. To be clear, such programs are great, and we should continue to explore ways to better share the gospel. However, so much emphasis in the New Testament is simply on Christians loving one another in the ways God has loved us in Christ. The "confidence" of the New Testament seems to be that when believers do so, it will attract unbelievers to faith. For example, when the apostles and deacons of the early church lived out their callings as a Christian community, people saw and "the number of disciples multiplied greatly in Jerusalem"—not only that, but "a great many of the [Jewish] priests became obedient to the faith" (Acts 6:7).

"There's something about community that draws people into a relationship with Jesus. One man on his own couldn't have brought this man to Jesus. Two men probably couldn't have carried him all the way. It took a community, a brotherhood, a small group."[14]

"Playing" Community

Many Christians would agree that community is important. But this is what tends to happen: they master the art of participating in community without actually engaging community. They go to church, become members, join a small group, and serve in different ways. And yet, they're able to keep people at a very safe distance. They don't know people deeply nor are they known deeply. They keep people from pursuing them by giving the appearance of being involved. Christian counselor Paul David Tripp observed this in his own life:

> No one helped my father to see through the blindness that allowed him to live a double life of skilled deception and duplicity. No one knew how troubled my mother was beneath her encyclopedic knowledge of Scripture. No one knew. We were a Christian family in active participation in a vibrant church . . .[15]

This makes sense to us—keeping people distant by keeping them near. Opening yourself up is scary because it makes you vulnerable. The reality is that the church is full of broken people. The gospel highlights that Jesus draws to himself the disenfranchised and abused, which includes those who have been hurt and will therefore hurt others. This is why Christians often compare the church to a spiritual hospital. In such a context, hurt is inevitable.

Years ago, I spoke at a youth retreat. There was a group of twenty girls who were divided into two rooms. When the girls rushed to the two rooms, nineteen of them went into one room and left a Post-It note on the door of the other room. This note was

14. Zempel, *Community Is Messy*, 15.

15. Tripp, *Dangerous Calling*, 83.

written for the "runt" of the group and read: "Haha, you ugly fart. You're going to sleep by yourself because no one wants to be your friend." The church can be a very cruel place. That's why when my non-Christian friends say, "Christians can be so mean," I respond, "You're right. That's why Jesus said, 'I came not to call the righteous but sinners'" (Mark 2:17).

So all this is understandable, but here C. S. Lewis gives an important warning to those who "play" community:

> Love anything, and your heart will certainly be wrung and possibly be broken. If you want to make sure of keeping it intact, you must give your heart to no one, not even to an animal. Wrap it carefully round with hobbies and little luxuries; avoid all entanglements; lock it up safe in the casket or coffin of your selfishness. But in that casket—safe, dark, motionless, airless—it will change. It will not be broken; it will become unbreakable, impenetrable, irredeemable.[16]

By avoiding community because of inevitable hurt, we lose our humanity.

Some know what Lewis has in mind because "hobbies and little luxuries" describe perfectly their lives. Some say, "This is still preferable to the pain of delving into Christian fellowship." But the gospel reminds us that deep participation in community is required *and* possible. First, it is required because salvation in Christ has both forensic and familial components. On the one hand, God, the judge, declares you righteous. So now you're justified. On the other hand, the judge then comes down, places his robe on you, and says, "Now come home with me to my family." So now you are adopted. If you believe in this gospel, that in Christ you have been justified and adopted, there is no other option than to join his family.

The gospel also reminds us that the Spirit of Christ lives in us. Christ did not just risk his life but he also lost his life to bring us into fellowship with the Father. He did not stay a safe distance but surrendered his comforts and became a human to draw near to us. He loved people, especially his disciples, even when he knew

16. Lewis, *The Four Loves*, 121.

they would betray and abandon him. Finally, on the cross he did not curse his mockers but prayed on their behalf. His Spirit now abides in us and reminds us that had he stayed at a safe distance, we would have been without hope. As we meditate on this reality, the Spirit softens our hearts and changes us to love the family of Christ. The Spirit makes us people who begin to think first about others, to endure difficult persons in hope and love, and to identify with them in tangible and profound ways.

God's purpose in our life is to work good (Rom 8:28); however, this "good" is not making all our hopes and dreams come true but making us more like Jesus Christ. This cannot happen so long as we keep people at a safe distance. We become more like Christ when we learn to love in the way he has loved us. We deepen in our appreciation for all he has done when we try to do the same. For this reason, we need community in order to become what we cannot become through "my personal relationship with Christ."

I emphasize this point of *needing* community because often our refusal to reconcile stems from the quiet belief that "I don't need the wrongdoer." In fact, we often suppose that our lives would be much better without that person. There might be some truth to the belief that life would be easier, but that doesn't mean life will be better. It's possible that God has placed you in fellowship with difficult or simply different believers in order to mature you into the image of Christ. When we are tempted to say, "I really don't need that person, and my life would be so much better without him," we need to recall that God's design is for us to know his will by being in fellowship, not just with those whom we like but also—and especially—with those whom God in his wisdom has ordained to be our brothers and sisters in faith.

Our Responsibility toward Community

In verse 7, Paul says to Philemon: "For I have derived much joy and comfort from your love, my brother, because the hearts of the saints have been refreshed through you."[17] In the Bible, the "heart" means much more than your emotions and feelings. It refers to the inner seat of the whole personality, our core affections. The heart is why we do what we do. It reflects the essence of who we are because it contains our deepest and most controlling love.[18]

Pastor Tim Keller regularly gives this illustration.[19] When he was a pastor in Hopewell, Virginia, there was a high school girl struggling with depression. He counseled her, saying: "Don't you know that Jesus died for you? Don't you know that nothing can separate you from God's love? Don't you know that someday you're destined for glory?" She responded: "Yeah, but what good is any of that if boys are not interested in me?" Keller explains that this young lady knew the truths of the gospel without having her heart enraptured by them.

This describes many faithful church attendees today. Though we know that Jesus died for all our sins and that the best is yet to come, we still brood. "Does any of this matter? I'm still single!" "My marriage stinks!" "I hate my job!" Deep down on the level of the "heart," there remains a deeper affection that still reigns—the approval of others, personal comfort, financial security, and so forth. So when Paul says that "the hearts of the saints have been refreshed through you," he's saying something very profound:

---

17. It is important to note that Paul's familial language ("brother") is not a "fictive kinship" as some suggest. Much rather, Paul's language is literal, a kinship that is real through the blood of Christ. See my comments in *1 Timothy, Vol. 1*, 73–74.

18. Longenecker comments on verse 7: "The word 'heart' is not the Greek word *kardia*, which occurs fifty-two times in the Pauline corpus, but the word *splanchnon*, which occurs only eight times in the Pauline corpus, three of which are in Philemon . . . In those occurrences, it usually connotes affection or compassion, referring to the seat of emotions" ("Philemon," 171). Moo observes similarly and identifies the significance that Paul intends with the word *splanchnon*: "in Philemon it has the former sense, 'the total personality at the deepest level.' Paul uses this word to stress that Philemon's love had 'refreshed' the people of God at the deepest and most significant level of their being" (*Letters*, 396).

19. E.g., Keller, "Excerpts from a Sermon," 4.

Philemon's ministry has changed the deepest loves and aspirations of the believers in his house.[20]

Paul reminds Philemon of his influence because he is about to make a difficult request. He is about to ask Philemon to forgive Onesimus and embrace him as a brother in the Lord. Paul is sure that Philemon's response will have repercussions on other believers because of his track record. For this reason, he reminds Philemon of his influence and therefore of his responsibility with respect to his community: whatever Philemon does—or doesn't do—will establish a culture and pattern for all the other believers to follow.

While we cannot save the world—it is *not* our duty to do so—we all have a deep impact on the spheres of influence that God has placed in our lives. This is what Paul is saying to Philemon. Even though Philemon has been wronged, if he doesn't accept and embrace Onesimus, all those people under his influence will learn to do likewise.[21] In verse 7 Paul is basically saying: "Look at what a force you are—the hearts of the saints have been so affected by your ministry. Given this . . ."

20. Moo, *Letters*, 396: "'Refresh' translates a word that Paul uses elsewhere in a very similar sense, to refer to the heartening and encouraging effect that effective ministry has on people (1 Cor. 16:18; 2 Cor. 7:13). Many ministries can appear to be successful but have, in fact, only a superficial and therefore very temporary impact on believers. Philemon's influence was not like that."

21. The biblical theme of imitation is pervasive throughout Paul's letters. As New Testament scholar Morna D. Hooker relates in her essay "A Partner in the Gospel," when Christians are to follow the pattern of Christ, "there is a sense in which Christians are called to imitate him . . . the notion of imitation is much more significant in Pauline thought than has often been allowed . . . More often than not, of course, Paul points to *himself* as the pattern for others to follow . . . But why does he set himself up as a pattern for other believers to imitate? The answer is set out most clearly in 1 Cor 11:1, where Paul urges the Corinthians to become imitators of him, *even as he is an imitator of Christ* . . . in other words, they are to be fellow-imitators with one another" (92–93).

What We Do Matters

Everything we say and do—and everything we don't say and don't do—impacts our community. This is seen especially in parenting. J. C. Ryle challenges parents to consider their effect on their children.

> *Train them remembering continually the influence of your own example.* Instruction, and advice, and commands, will profit little, unless they are backed up by the pattern of your own life. Your children will never believe you are in earnest, and really wish them to obey you, so long as your actions contradict your counsel. Archbishop Tillotson made a wise remark, when he said, "To give children good instruction, and a bad example, is but beckoning to them with the head to show them the way to heaven, while we take them by the hand, and lead them in the way to Hell."[22]

Ryle goes on to say this:

> We little know the force and power of example. No one of us can live to himself in this world; we are always influencing those around us, in one way or another, either for good or for evil, either for God or for sin . . . Fathers and Mothers, do not forget that children learn more by the eye than they do by the ear. Imitation is a far stronger principle with them than memory. What they see has a much stronger effect on their minds than what they are told. Take care then what you do before a child. It is a true proverb, "Who sins before a child sins double." . . . Think not your children will practise what they do not see you do. You are their model picture, and they will copy what you are. Your reasoning and your lecturing, your wise commands and your good advice;—all this they may not understand, but they can understand your life . . . Remember the word that the conqueror Caesar always used to his soldiers in a battle. He did not say, "*Go* forward" but "*Come.*" So it must be with you in training your children.[23]

22. Ryle, "Train Up a Child," 50–51.
23. Ibid., 51–53.

While Ryle is speaking specifically about parenting, the general principle of influence applies to every realm: your life and decisions are not inconsequential on the lives of others.

Some might think, "Well, I've had nothing but bad examples in my life." Maybe you had bad parents, or maybe you didn't have parents. But even then, Paul says that we can follow the pattern of the gospel. In Ephesians 4:32, he writes: "Be kind to one another, tenderhearted, forgiving one another, as God in Christ forgave you." We have not been left as orphans. God has given us the Spirit of Christ who continues to point us to the One who has modeled for us the kind of life we are to live as his disciples.

As Ryle suggests, we must be sober to the fact that we are always either pointing people toward heaven or hell. Parents must be sober to the reality that even if your child lacks the ability to understand everything you say and do, from a young age they can figure out what matters to you.[24] Even the desire to live a quiet and "safe" life is not inconsequential. You don't get involved with others but keep a distance. That speaks volumes to your children. Unconsciously, you're promoting a life of self-preservation. Therefore, wherever you are, whether you're with your church family or individual family, you need to ask the question of intentionality: are you demonstrating what it means to follow Christ? Is your life pointing people toward grace and glory? Is your life refreshing the hearts of the saints?

Concerning reconciliation, this point of our influence and responsibility toward the saints is regularly forgotten. When we are in conflict, we think of it in personal ways: the conflict is strictly between me and another party. We fail to realize the impact that

---

24. Tripp, *Parenting*, 24–25: "Here's what you need to understand: everything you do and say in your life, every choice that you make, and everything you decide to invest in is a reflection of a system of internalized values in your heart . . . Your words, your time commitments, your finances, your emotional highs and lows, your relationships, and your spiritual habits together form a portrait of what is really valuable to you. Think with me for a moment; if I were to watch with you the video of your last two months, what would I conclude is of true value to you?" That "video" is what our kids watch; from it, they learn what is of true value.

broken relationships have on the greater community. In his comments on verse 2, Moo offers these helpful insights:

> By making the issue of Onesimus a public one, Paul increases the pressure on Philemon to respond as he wishes. But we should not view the public nature of the letter as simply a lawyer's tactic to win his case; it rather reflects the corporate nature of early Christianity, in which no matter was "private" but inevitably affected, and was affected by, one's brothers and sisters in the new family of God.[25]

A refusal to reconcile creates a culture where unreconciled relationships become the new norm. In the process, there is usually gossip, slander, and a loss in focus on our call to share the gospel and abound in good works. Also, there are so many opportunity costs: the relationships that could have formed and the synergy that could have been are lost as a result of division and bitterness. As members of God's missional household, we bear the corporate responsibility of seeking reconciliation in order to facilitate unity, evangelism, and good works.

Summary

Faith in the Lord Jesus cannot be separated from a deep love for the people of Christ. To claim to love God but to fail to love those for whom he died doesn't make any sense. It's like saying to your fiancé, "I love you, but I want nothing to do with all the people you have ever loved." Also, to be saved means to be adopted. As we have noted above, this means that we both need the communion of saints and are needed by them. To have love for the saints means being willing to humble ourselves and acknowledge our dependence on them. Similarly, to love the saints means fulfilling the unique role to which God has called us for the upbuilding of the entire body of Christ. All this might sound basic, but in our individualistic age we need continual reminders of this new reality in Christ. We were built to live in and for community.

25. Moo, *Letters*, 383–84.

This high view of community is foundational for understanding the Bible's view on reconciliation. When we discern that Christ died not just to reconcile us to God but also to one another, and when we realize our complementary dependence on the body of Christ and our responsibility to them, reconciliation seems more sensible. I would argue that so much of why we don't reconcile is because we believe—unconsciously or not—that we don't really need other believers or that we need a few (the ones we like). If, however, we believe that God has surrounded us with the "right" believers—those who will sanctify us in the ways he has ordained to be good and necessary—we will prioritize reconciliation.

3

Peacemaking

Philemon 8–22

HAVING CONSIDERED THE BASIC building blocks of identity and community as well as the role they play in reconciliation, we now turn our attention to the body of the letter (vv. 8–22). Here, Paul makes his appeal to Philemon, asking him to be reconciled with Onesimus. Noteworthy is his winsome approach to the delicate situation. As an apostle, he is in a position "to command [Philemon] to do what is required" (v. 8). But he takes a circuitous route "for love's sake" (v. 9). In doing so, he shows by example the hard work involved in facilitating peace: we must go the extra step of thinking through situations and developing the best strategy to achieve peace.[1]

The body of this letter is full of insights, but we will limit our reflections to just four. First, we see the vital role that intervention plays in reconciliation. Second, we consider the gospel dynamic behind Paul's counsel to Philemon. Third, we give attention to the inescapable condition of blindness that plagues every believer at every stage of maturing in Christ. Finally, we touch on the subject of effective gospel persuasion.

---

1. Migliore, *Philippians and Philemon*, 203: "As this letter demonstrates, Paul is not only a stalwart proclaimer but also an exemplary practitioner of the gospel of reconciliation and new life in Christ."

The Role of Mediation in Reconciliation[2]

We tend to think of reconciliation in personal ways: "I must reconcile with my enemies, with those that have wronged me." In a sense, this is fitting given the main person we are responsible for is the self. Still, in this short letter we see the critical role that intervention plays in facilitating reconciliation: had Paul not interceded for Onesimus, the chances for reconciliation would have dropped exponentially.

All of us are aware of some broken relationship. It may be related to family, church, or the workplace. But we choose not to get involved. This is understandable because conflicts are messy, and who wants to make life more complicated than it is? Anyone that has ever tried to mediate a conflict can attest to this. It's not easy standing between two parties. Often one, if not both parties, will get upset at the mediator. Life is just easier "minding your own business." The problem is that the "business" of unreconciled relationships among believers is our business. As we have highlighted in the prior chapters of this book, God has brought us into his family. Therefore, what affects his family affects us. We need to get involved in order to facilitate peace even as Jesus got "involved" to make peace between God and man. To remain passive is to commit the sin of omission.

The phenomenon of unreconciled relationships has become the new norm. And whether we are willing to admit it, we have played a role in this. Some have failed to pursue reconciliation in their own lives. Others have remained passive—"not wanting to take sides." The typical justification is, "I'm just too busy with more pressing items." This justification is probably not entirely untrue. But given the Bible's emphasis and priority on facilitating peace, it is hard to imagine many things more important than helping to create a culture of peacemaking. It's not as if the apostle Paul had nothing better to do in prison and therefore decided to assist Onesimus during his downtime. All his letters indicate that facilitating peace was a priority because the gospel is all about the restoration of broken relationships.

2. For a helpful supplement, see Sande's section on mediation and arbitration in *Peacemaker* (26, 271–72).

For Paul to make peace between Philemon and Onesimus, he had to pray, think through an effective strategy, pen a thoughtful letter, remind Philemon of basic gospel truths, and commit to accountability. In other words, serving as a mediator required a lot of work. Nevertheless, he knew that if he did not intervene, his two "sons" would remain unreconciled and the church in Philemon's house would have moved further from developing a culture of peace. Thus for the sake of Christ and the church, Paul stepped into the messiness. In like fashion, if we are serious about bucking the trend toward unreconciled relationships, we must be serious about pursuing reconciled relationships in our personal lives and in the lives of others. At the risk of promoting savior complexes, there is something right about the belief, "Unless I get involved here, reconciliation probably won't happen."

The Gospel Dynamic of Paul's Counsel

The Letter to Philemon is not as theologically robust as Galatians or Romans. Yet, it is not devoid of doctrinal instruction. Key topics like ecclesiology (doctrine of the church) and imputation (doctrine of salvation) are assumed in Paul's counsel to Philemon. In fact, these doctrines form the basis for why Philemon should have a new outlook on life. The language of "formerly . . . but now" in verse 11 captures the essence of this new outlook. As we mature in Christ, more and more our lives should reflect the dynamism of "formerly . . . but now": "Formerly I thought and responded like this. But now—because of Christ—I think and respond in a new way." Let's consider two ways these doctrines challenge Philemon.

First, the Bible's teaching on ecclesiology changes the way we relate to people in general but especially to believers. "Formerly" Onesimus had the social status of a "bondservant"—literally, a "slave" (v. 16). "But now" Onesimus is a "beloved brother."[3] Hence, though his social status was the same, his fundamental identity is different. No longer is he an object of wrath; now he is a coheir of glory. Also, as a member of God's household, he is now Paul's "child" in the faith (v. 10), Philemon's "beloved brother" (v. 16), and their partner for the gospel (vv. 11, 13, 17). In sum, irrespective of the former personal grievance between Philemon and Onesimus, now they are family in the Lord Jesus. The only response consistent with this gospel reality is for Philemon to "receive him as you would receive me" (v. 17).

Old habits are hard to break. This holds true especially in the way we engage people. We're trained to engage people "according to the flesh." That is, unconsciously—and very quickly—we size people up and engage them in like fashion. If a person is prestigious, then we'll be on our best behavior. We'll be fully engaged in the conversation, we'll make eye contact, and we'll make every effort to give a positive impression. But if the person doesn't seem to offer much in the way of advancing our personal and professional goals, it's unlikely that we'll offer them our time and undivided attention.

The Christian faith challenges us to be purposeful about adopting a new perspective. C. S. Lewis said it best:

> It is a serious thing to live in a society of possible gods and goddesses, to remember that the dullest and most uninteresting person you can talk to may one day be a creature which, if you saw it now, you would be strongly tempted to worship, or else a horror and a corruption such as you now meet, if at all, only in a nightmare . . . There are no *ordinary* people. You have never talked to a mere mortal. Nations, cultures, arts, civilisations—these are mortal, and their life is to ours as the life of a gnat. But it is immortals whom we joke with, work with, marry, snub, and exploit—immortal horrors or everlasting splendours.[4]

---

3. As Still comments: "Linguistically, Paul signals this reversal by employing the contrastive pairing 'once or formerly' (*pote*) 'but now' (*nuni de*). He employs this antithesis to juxtapose individuals' pre-Christian state with their current Christian standing" (*Philippians & Philemon*, 173).

4. Lewis, *Weight of Glory*, 45.

All people merit respect because all people are God's image-bearers. But all who belong to God's household merit a special kind of love and devotion, the sort we give to our family. They are our family in the Lord. Hence, the apostle Paul exhorts: "So then, as we have opportunity, let us do good to everyone, and especially to those who are of the household of faith" (Gal 6:10). With them we will sing God's eternal praises in the new heaven and the new earth. Therefore, the gospel calls us to set aside our former ways of engaging believers—according to the flesh—and to now receive and embrace them as family and coheirs of glory. Failure to do so pushes us down the slope of forgetting who they are in Christ and, in turn, who we are.

This principle sounds basic, but so easily we lose sight of its many applications. I live in the Washington, D.C. area where there are many sincere believers with very different political commitments. One question I get asked often is how Christians are to engage other Christians who have very different political commitments. A weighty and nuanced answer could be given.[5] But at the risk of sounding simplistic, it helps to keep in mind the basic doctrine of the church. Too often I hear each side vilify the other. Believers who are Republicans accuse believers who are Democrats of compromising their faith and being naïve about humanity's ability to make the world a better place. Believers who are Democrats accuse believers who are Republicans of being narrow-minded and backward in their thinking. Eventually both sides disdain the other and minimize their interaction to mere formalities. To both groups the gospel says not to view the other as "Republican" or "Democrat" but as Christian—as fellow members of God's household, partners for the gospel, and coheirs of Christ's glory. I suspect that placing this identity at the forefront of our engagement with believers of differing political ideologies will foster greater fellowship.

5. See, e.g., "Jesus and Your Political Party" by Duke Kwon. Along with Kwon, Tim Keller asserts: "We might start getting divided politically instead of remembering that you're Christian first and you're white, black, Asian, Hispanic, second. You're a Christian first and you're American, or you're British and you're African second" (Blair, "Tim Keller Warns Christians").

Second, the Bible's teaching on salvation changes the way we pursue forgiveness and reconciliation. Verse 18 reads: "If [Onesimus] has wronged you at all, or owes you anything, charge that to my account." There are three persons in view: Paul the mediator, Onesimus the guilty, and Philemon the judge. Basically, Paul says to Philemon, "Treat me as if I had wronged you—'charge that to my account'—and receive Onesimus as you would me" (v. 17). It is unlikely that Philemon would have missed the underlying doctrine. According to the gospel, there are three parties: Jesus the mediator, humanity the guilty, and God the righteous judge. Basically, Jesus says to God the Father: "Treat me as if I had sinned—'charge that to my account'—and receive those who trust in me as if they had obeyed perfectly." Indeed, elsewhere the apostle writes: "For our sake he made him to be sin who knew no sin, so that in him we might become the righteousness of God" (2 Cor 5:21).

To be sure, Onesimus had wronged Philemon. Nowhere in the letter does Paul seek to minimize this. However, Paul wants Philemon to adopt a new perspective on how to respond to personal situations of conflict and hurt. "Formerly" Philemon would have responded very much in the way he's currently responding. He would have demanded justice. He might have sought vengeance. If neither was possible, at the very least he would have harbored bitterness, possibly dreaming of ways to get back at Onesimus. At every opportunity, he would have spoken ill of his perpetrator. "But now" Philemon must consider a response that accords with the gospel.

This very idea of "charge that to my account" recalls the famous "Parable of the Good Samaritan" (Luke 10:25–37). Not only does the Samaritan draw near to the dying man, he also binds the man's wounds, sets him on his own animal, and brings him to an inn to receive additional care. The parable ends with these words: "And the next day he took out two denarii and gave them to the innkeeper, saying, 'Take care of him, and whatever more you spend, I will repay you when I come back'" (Luke 10:35). In other words, the Samaritan tells the innkeeper to "charge that to my account."[6] Of course, this parable is really about what Christ has done for us. Christ places himself in danger, heals us of our brokenness, and forfeits his wealth to make us well. Having received such mercy from God the judge and Christ the mediator, Philemon must consider how he will respond to Onesimus now that he stands in the position of judge with Paul as the mediator.

We should highlight that forgiveness is not optional. The personal and somewhat gentle tone of Paul's appeal might leave the impression that Paul was merely making a suggestion that Philemon could choose to disregard. But this is mistaken. At the outset of the body of the letter, Paul writes that he is indeed "bold enough in Christ to command you to do what is required" (v. 8). The language here is unambiguous: Philemon must forgive Onesimus because that is "what is required" of all believers.

Sometimes we get uncomfortable with this kind of "requirement" language. The gospel, after all, declares that we are saved by grace, not by our works. While it is true that we are saved by faith

6. For a fuller treatment of this parable, see Keller, *Ministries of Mercy*, who spells out the implications here of "charge that to my account": "Nevertheless, in opposition to all these forces, the Samaritan had 'compassion' (v. 33). This compassion was full-bodied, leading him to meet a variety of needs. This compassion provided friendship and advocacy, emergency medical treatment, transportation, a hefty financial subsidy, and even a follow-up visit . . . Our paradigm is the Samaritan, who risked his safety, destroyed his schedule, and became dirty and bloody through personal involvement with a needy person of another race and social class" (13).

alone, our faith is in Jesus Christ our Lord (Rom 1:4). Trusting in Jesus for salvation, then, cannot be separated from submitting to him as our master.[7] And it is this master who gave us the "Parable of the Unforgiving Servant" that ends on the sobering note: "Then his master summoned him and said to him, 'You wicked servant! I forgave you all that debt because you pleaded with me. And should not you have had mercy on your fellow servant, as I had mercy on you?'" (Matt 18:32–33). For reasons we will discuss below, Paul avoids using such direct and forceful language. But Paul's careful diction and thoughtful persuasion is meant to convey the same rebuke: the gospel of mercy must profoundly reshape our former way of responding to hurt and conflict.

Our Inescapable Blindness

It might serve our reflections on this particular point to take a step back and recall how extraordinary Philemon was as a leader. We get some hints throughout the letter:

- Paul considers him a "beloved fellow worker" (v. 1).

- Philemon is generous with his home: he excels in hospitality (v. 2).

- Philemon has genuine faith in the Lord as evidenced by his love for the saints (v. 5).

- Philemon's ministry has had a profound impact on the lives of other believers (v. 7).

In sum, Philemon was a commendable leader, a pillar of faith, a worthy model. Also, it was not uncommon for the "master of the house" to serve as its overseer.[8] Thus we can surmise that Phile-

7. Gorman, *Cruciformity*, 261: "For Philemon, failing to obey Paul here . . . would be a decision to undo the decision he made at baptism irrevocably to put on the story of Christ and to allow all of his relationships to be governed by the lordship of Christ."

8. Commenting on Paul's description of "overseers" in 1 Timothy 3, Aubrey Malphurs writes: "While the term *overseer* is used here and not *pastor*, the overseers or elders were the first-century house church pastors who were the

mon was the functional pastor for the believers that met in his home and taught them the doctrines Paul alludes to in the letter.

Why is it, then, that Paul must counsel him on basic truths of the gospel and their implications?[9] Notice the concern here isn't some heresy involving trinitarian doctrine or differences in ministry philosophy. Paul's appeal in verse 15 boils down to this: "Onesimus is a believer, you're a believer. Come on—get an eternal perspective on this!" What important lesson can we learn? Our inescapable blindness! Was Philemon taken aback by any of Paul's counsel? Did it escape his mind that in Christ we are one and that we ought to forgive as Christ has forgiven us? Probably not. Yet, despite his deep theological knowledge and his ability to apply it effectively to the lives of others, he was unable to discern his own failure to apply the gospel to his current and personal situation. Tripp identifies sin as the main culprit of this blindness:

> Sin is deceptive, and think with me about who it deceives first. I have no difficulty recognizing the sin of the people around me, but I can be quite unprepared when my sin is pointed out. Sin deceives ten out of ten people reading this book . . . spiritually blind people are not only blind; they are blind to their own blindness.[10]

I have the privilege to serve both as a pastor and a seminary professor. My regular work life involves studying the Bible carefully, reading theology, and staying aware of trends in biblical studies. Church members regularly come to me for advice on how to handle various situations in a way that accords with the gospel. Similarly, seminary students will often interrupt me in the middle of a lecture to ask how they can apply a seemingly esoteric theological truth to "real" life. Given the natural pride of the heart that inclines us to think highly and frequently about ourselves, I and people in similar situations are especially susceptible to the

---

approximate equivalent of today's pastors" (*Nuts and Bolts*, 188).

9. Peterson highlights the irony: "Paul addresses Philemon first because he is both the church's leader and its problem, and those are the facts that are fundamental to Paul's letter and story" (*Rediscovering Paul*, 298).

10. Tripp, *Dangerous Calling*, 73.

belief that we have "arrived" and therefore see all and know all. To be sure, few pastors, counselors, and teachers will ever make such explicit statements. But such pride shows its ugly face when we become unduly sensitive to and dismissive of criticism and allow unreconciled relationships to persist in our lives. The safest disposition to adopt is that of a perennial student, readily acknowledging our blind spots and always being open to hearing the counsel of men and women who care for our souls.[11]

Indeed, God's basic remedy for the blinding power of sin is community. As we noted in our comments on verse 6, we can never fully know ourselves in abstraction and isolation. In fact, more often than not, we tend to entertain lofty views of ourselves! "The blinding ability of sin is so powerful and persuasive that you and I literally need daily intervention . . . Each of us, whether pastor or congregant, needs the eyes of others in order to see ourselves with clarity and accuracy."[12] Not unlike Philemon, without the insight and help of community, we will either fall short of personal gospel application or remain indifferent to our shortcomings.

Effective Gospel Persuasion

When studying this letter, many focus on the theme of reconciliation. No doubt this is an important theme as it captures Paul's main purpose. But a second and third review of the letter suggest another important takeaway—effective gospel persuasion.[13] Perhaps

11. We observed this in the previous chapter, but the point can't be overstated. Professor Victor I. Ezigbo is spot-on: "Christians need each other to become aware of the threat or presence of sin. Our spiritual blind spots, which are conditioned by our cultures and personal experiences, may prevent us from seeing a potential circumstance in which we may be led to sin" (*Introducing Christian Theologies*, 325).

12. Tripp, *Dangerous Calling*, 73. Mike McKinley similarly observes: "Becoming a Christian means admitting that you are a sinner, and admitting that you are [a] sinner means admitting that you are prone to self-deceit. Gratefully, God has given us other Christians to help us see the things we cannot see about ourselves" (*Am I Really a Christian?*, 16).

13. As Witherington observes: "But at the outset we must emphasize that understanding what Paul is saying and trying to accomplish in this letter

our focus, then, should be as much on the theme of persuasion as on reconciliation. One might be tempted to dismiss Paul's style of communication as passive-aggressive. But a more careful reflection reveals its winsome quality.[14] In fact, it's been pointed out that Paul's Letter to Philemon "is a masterpiece of Greek persuasion."[15]

As a whole the Bible places a premium on thoughtful communication. Perhaps the most well-known example is Nathan's confrontation with king David. David had committed adultery with Uriah's wife and had him killed. What made this crime especially heinous was that Uriah had served as a personal guard and friend to David. Nevertheless, when Nathan the prophet approaches David, he does not come outright and declare David a wicked sinner. Instead, he shares with David a graphic and moving story (2 Sam 12:1–6). The sum and substance of the story is that a rich man steals "one little ewe lamb" from a poor man to feed his out-of-town guests (12:3). The prophet highlights that this little lamb "was a like a daughter" to the poor man (12:3). Upon hearing this story, "David's anger was greatly kindled," and he declared, "As the Lord lives, the man who has done this deserves to die" (12:5). It's at this point Nathan declares, "You are the man!" (12:7).

This confrontation would have likely ended differently if Nathan had adopted a more direct approach. Suppose he had asked

---

depends to some degree on recognizing how he is using the art of persuasion" (*Letters*, 51). Similarly, Moo writes: "The heart of the letter body is Paul's 'appeal' for Onesimus (v. 10). Paul, however, does not spell out the specifics of his appeal explicitly until v. 17, where he asks Philemon to 'welcome' Onesimus. Paul delays this specific request until then because he is pursuing a rhetorical strategy of persuasion" (*Letters*, 398).

14. Again, Witherington's comments are apt, distinguishing between divinely inspired gospel persuasion versus merely passive-aggressive tactics: "Before we disparage rhetoric, we would do well to realize that it is the main weapon in our arsenal, for it is the divinely ordained means of evangelizing the world, discipling the saints, and leading congregations in the paths of righteousness. Rhetoric, as it turns out, is not the real manipulation. That comes when people try to bypass or circumvent persuasion and attempt to accomplish things by strong arm tactics, secret meanings, and other sorts of passive-aggressive behavior" (*Letters*, 97).

15. Burtchaell, *Philemon's Problem*, 11.

David, "Is there something you want to talk about?" or begun with the statement, "I know what you did!" Immediately, David would have been on the defensive and might have even responded with violence and irrationality. As many effective communicators have noted, the basic principle is: "You need to let people arrive at the right conclusion on their own. Your job is to guide them there." That's what Nathan did. And that's what Paul is trying to achieve. By adopting an indirect but clear approach, Paul wants Philemon to see the profound implications of refusing to forgive Onesimus. How can Philemon refuse to receive Onesimus given that Jesus has forgiven him? Also, Paul wants Philemon to be sober about the impact this unreconciled relationship will have on the entire church that meets in his house. But all this he wants Philemon to arrive at through an appeal versus a command.

There are four aspects of Paul's gospel persuasion with Philemon that we want to highlight.[16] His communication is humble, personal, reasonable, and accountable.

Humble Communication

First, Paul's appeal exudes humility. As an apostle, Paul could have commanded Philemon "to do what is required" (v .8) with the expectation of full submission. Also, he could have kept Onesimus "that he might serve me on your behalf during my imprisonment for the gospel" (v. 13). In other words, it would have been advantageous for Paul to keep Onesimus instead of sending him back. But Paul surrenders both his rights and preferences for Philemon's sake. This overall disposition is striking given that Philemon is Paul's debtor, having come to faith through the apostle's ministry (v. 19). In general, when we approach individuals with a disposition marked not by positional authority ("command," v. 8) but by love and humility, people are more willing to engage in reconciliatory dialogue.[17]

16. For supplemental discussion, see the entire chapter "Speak the Truth in Love" in Sande's *Peacemaker* regarding the work of effective, careful persuasion (162–84).

17. Here we do have to be careful about absolutizing any single principle.

Personal Communication

Second, Paul's appeal is profoundly personal. Even a cursory read of the letter makes clear that Philemon and the apostle enjoy an intimate relationship, enough so that the apostle can make bold requests (vv. 20, 22). Notice also how Paul uses deeply personal imagery: "I, Paul, an old man and now a prisoner also for Christ Jesus" (v. 9); "I appeal to you for my child, Onesimus, whose father I became in my imprisonment" (v. 10); "I am sending him back to you, sending my very heart" (v. 12). What is Paul doing here? He is "cashing in" on the relational mileage he has earned with Philemon. Paul has invested so much "life" in Philemon that he knows Philemon cannot be indifferent to Paul's plight and plea. Onesimus is no longer just a person that has wronged Philemon; he is Paul's spiritual "child," his very "heart." To disregard Onesimus would be akin to your best friend having little regard for your son! There is little doubt that both Philemon and the church would have missed the personal nature of continuing to refuse Onesimus into the fellowship of saints: such a rejection would be an affront to Paul himself. For this reason, Paul writes, "So if you *consider me your partner*, receive him as you would receive me" (v. 17).

But the care goes both ways. Paul expresses his care for Philemon both explicitly and implicitly. As noted already, he indicates that he could "command you to do what is required, yet for love's sake . . ." (v. 8b–9). This makes clear Paul's personal affection for his fellow worker Philemon. Similarly, he writes concerning Onesimus, "I would have been glad to keep him . . . but I preferred to do nothing without your consent" (vv. 13–14a). In other words, Paul thinks first of the needs and preferences of Philemon over his own. More implicitly Paul expresses care for Philemon by conveying concern for his heart: "but I preferred to do nothing without your consent in order that your goodness might not be by compulsion but of your own accord" (v. 14). Paul doesn't want "resigned submission" but action based on a heart-change on Philemon's part.

Wisdom dictates that there are instances when direct and forceful language is fitting. This same apostle also penned Galatians. In that letter, he skips his characteristic prayer of thanksgiving and refers to the Galatians as fools (3:1).

In a sense, it would have been easier for Paul to simply command Philemon to do something and threaten punishment if he refused to do so. But he knew that such "obedience" would be just behavioral and fail to address the underlying heart issues. Thus, in verse 14 Paul expresses his concern not only for the situation at hand but also for the spiritual state of Philemon's heart.

In passing, this specific point about communication reminds us of the relational groundwork involved behind actual communication. That is, a person's credibility has a direct impact on the listener's receptivity. A person that is loved and respected by the listener will have a greater audience than a stranger, especially when it comes to difficult words. If we want people to listen, whether we are coming in as a teacher, preacher, mediator, or counselor, we need to first do the hard work of investing in people.[18] This isn't to suggest that relational investment in people is purely a means to an end. Rather, we need to be sober about the reality that in general people who feel loved and cherished are much more inclined to receive encouragement, rebuke, and exhortation.

Reasonable Communication

Third, Paul's communication is intended to engage Philemon's sensibilities. Of course, he assumes here the background of the gospel, which is the only way to appreciate the rationality of Paul's argument. In verses 15–16 he suggests: "For this perhaps is why he was parted from you for a while, that you might have him back forever, no longer as a bondservant but more than a bondservant, as a beloved brother—especially to me, but how much more to you, both in the flesh and in the Lord." Again, this makes sense only from an eternal perspective. To be sure, Philemon has suffered some significant loss because of Onesimus. At the same time, from the perspective of the gospel, so much more has been gained—the least of which is Onesimus's salvation. Somehow God used this tragedy to

18. As psychologists Jeff and Nancy Cochran observe: "Counseling can never lack investment of the counselor's emotion and energy . . . The best and most efficient counseling is 'heartfelt'" (*Heart of Counseling*, 1).

accomplish more good than anything either Paul or Philemon could have imagined. In this sense, Paul is reasoning with Philemon from a cost-benefit analysis: "Yes, in the short-run you suffered. But consider how God providentially used this occasion not just to restore Onesimus to you but also—and all the more—to his Creator and Redeemer. So now you have him back, 'no longer as a bondservant but more than a bondservant, as a beloved brother.'"

To the "natural mind" this line of reasoning does not hold any weight. But to those who are being saved, what Paul says here and elsewhere in the letter is perfectly reasonable. From a natural perspective, it makes little sense to receive people like Onesimus who, frankly speaking, have little to offer. They do not advance our socio-economic standing. They seem to have a track record of creating trouble. They run away from the problems they've created instead of taking ownership. It makes no sense to embrace them. But from the perspective of the gospel, it makes perfect sense. In fact, it "is required" (v. 8). Again, hear Paul's words in Ephesians: "Be kind to one another, tenderhearted, forgiving one another, as God in Christ forgave you" (4:32). Paul's communication, then, is reasonable because it flows from a mutual acceptance of the gospel and a common commitment to follow Jesus.

For believers in particular, the decision to live in an unreconciled state represents a failure to think deeply enough about the situation (or just plain disobedience). Paul suggests this in three ways. The first we have already noted elsewhere. Onesimus is not merely Philemon's bondservant who has wronged him and run away. Now, through Paul's ministry, he is a son to the apostle (v. 10) and a brother to Philemon (v. 16). And all three are fellow servants of the Lord, redeemed and received through Christ's atoning work. Viewed from this perspective, it is inconceivable to continue to hold a grudge. A consistent outworking of salvation by grace and adoption into God's family requires reconciliation, or at least a willingness to do so. In this sense, a refusal to be reconciled represents unreasonable thinking.

A second example of the reasonable quality to Paul's communication approach is implicit in verses 18–19: "If he has wronged you at all, or owes you anything, charge that to my account. I, Paul, write this with my own hand: I will repay it—to say nothing of your owing me even your own self." Here Paul is obviously rehearsing the gospel. As sinners, all have "wronged" God, but instead of "charging that" to our "accounts," God "charges" our sins to Christ's "account" and thus treats him as if he had rebelled against God. We, in turn, our "charged" with Christ's obedience; thus God treats us as if we had perfectly loved and obeyed him.[19] In sum, Jesus "repaid it"—he paid for all our sins. Thus we "owe" to him our entire "selves." The only reasonable outworking of this gospel in Philemon's life would be to extend to Onesimus the grace he himself first received from the Father, Son, and Holy Spirit.

Third, and related to the last instance, is Paul's attempt to show Philemon that it is unreasonable for him to suppose that the Christian life is marked by complete equity (at least in this life). Believers maintain that someday Jesus will come to judge the world according to righteousness. This doesn't mean we should not pursue justice in this life, but it does mean that we believe full justice will not be met in this life.[20] This is implied in Paul's rhetorical questions in his correspondence with the Corinthians: "To have lawsuits at all with one another is already a defeat for you. Why not rather suffer wrong? Why not rather be defrauded?" (1 Cor 6:7). In a sense, Paul is saying to Philemon, "Perhaps it is the case he has wronged you. Even so, is it worth breaking fellowship and setting a poor example for all the other believers?" Christianity is not about tit for tat but about grace.

---

19. The best treatment of this idea of imputation is John Murray's *The Imputation of Adam's Sin*: "The one ground upon which the imputation of the righteousness of Christ becomes ours is the union with Christ. In other words, the justified person is constituted righteous by the obedience of Christ because of the solidarity established between Christ and the justified person" (70).

20. See my comments in *1 Timothy, Vol. 3*, 105–06.

Again, for this reason a refusal to reconcile represents a resolve to be out of accord with the gospel. If our basic disposition is to receive full payment and justice for the wrongs that have been committed against us, what are we to make of how God has forgiven and received us? A summons to be reconciled always stems from a consistent outworking of the gospel of grace.

Accountable Communication

The last aspect of Paul's gospel persuasion is his emphasis on accountability. Here too we can look at this aspect in three different ways. First, Paul makes clear what it means for Philemon to be reconciled to Onesimus: "So if you consider me your partner, receive him *as you would receive me*" (v. 17). A few verses later Paul spells out the treatment he himself expects: "prepare a guest room for me" (v. 22). This would have included not just a place to lodge but also food and intimate fellowship. Anyone that has ever hosted a person knows that you don't only provide a bed for your guest. You also carve out time to eat, catch up, laugh—in short, to reconnect and strengthen ties. By adding the qualifier "as you would receive me," Paul makes clear that he is not looking for merely inner forgiveness. Philemon is to express his receipt of Onesimus in tangible ways that express a desire for more than superficial fellowship.

Second, accountability is expressed in terms of summoning Philemon to live in step with the gospel. As we have noted above, by saying, "If he has wronged you at all, or owes you anything, charge that to my account" (v. 18), he is rehearsing the gospel for Philemon. We wronged God, but our sins are charged to Christ's account and his righteousness to ours. It is not enough for Philemon to possess this knowledge. The experience of such mercy in Christ Jesus ought to make him merciful to all, but especially to those who belong to the household of faith.

Finally, Paul tells Philemon: "prepare a guest room for me, for I am hoping that through your prayers I will be graciously given to you" (v. 22). This is not merely a personal request along the lines of, "Let me stay at your place when I'm released from prison." Rather, in no uncertain terms Paul is telling Philemon that he will likely be seeing the apostle face-to-face in the near future. At that time, it will either be refreshing to see how Philemon carried out Paul's pleas, or it will be incredibly awkward if Philemon has continued to hold a grudge against Onesimus. Paul, after all, has openly expressed his faith in Philemon: "Confident of your obedience, I write to you, knowing that you will do even more than I say" (v. 21). In short, verses 21–22 indicate that Paul will keep Philemon accountable—he will make sure that Philemon is walking in step with the gospel.[21]

Summary

For followers of Christ Jesus, there is no greater influence on the way we communicate than God's way of communicating to us. In the Old Testament, we see all these aspects of gospel persuasion in God's covenant-relationship with Israel. In Calvin's words, God humbly "babbles" in order to make himself intelligible;[22] he relates to his people in deeply personal ways; he reasons with his people;[23] and he holds them to covenant-accountability. In the New Testament, all four aspects are heightened. In Jesus we have the ultimate surrender of rights and preferences; in Jesus we have God becoming ultimately personal; in Jesus we have God's "rationale" for living good and upright lives; and in Jesus covenantal-faithfulness

21. Harrington, *Paul's Prison Letters*, 25–26: "By expressing his expectation that Philemon will comply with his request (21), Paul is not suddenly pulling rank and demanding obedience to his apostolic authority. Rather, obedience is owed to Christian faith expressed in loving deeds, not to Paul (see 6). However, by announcing his plans to visit Philemon's house in the near future (22), he certainly adds to the pressure. When he arrives, Paul will be able to see for himself what has happened with Onesimus."

22. T. H. L. Parker explains what Calvin means by God "babbles" to us: "Within the Trinity we must believe, communication is not conducted, say, by means of rabbinic arguments, nor in Hebrew, Greek, or Aramaic. Yet these human languages and some sort of rational argument are all that human beings can understand. Therefore God accommodates himself to man and expresses his mind in this 'babbling' so that he may communicate to him his purposes in Jesus Christ" (*Calvin's New Testament Commentaries*, 94–95).

23. Isaiah 1:18 reads: "Come now, let us reason together, says the Lord."

is fully realized. How can we not be loving when we have experienced God's love in such profound ways? If we know the God of redemption, the God who has revealed himself clearly and finally in the person of Christ Jesus, should we not be more thoughtful about the way we communicate? It is easy to base our communication practices on our personality or upbringing. The gospel calls us to be much more deliberate by considering the ways of persuasion that reflect the wisdom and grace we see in the Lord Jesus Christ.

Epilogue

"By this all people will know that you are my disciples, if you have love for one another."—John 13:35

EVEN AS I CONCLUDE this book, I think of the many broken relationships I'm aware of—broken relationships in my family, in my church, in my denomination. What's striking is that all these broken relationships involve Christians—those who would count themselves as serious believers and are fully given over to the work of the Lord. Indeed, many of them are busy doing very good work, promoting racial reconciliation, pastoring large churches, giving money to missionaries, and so forth. But they're also keenly aware of severed relationships and, to be plain, are doing little if anything to make peace. Somehow, many believers haven't gotten the memo and have come to believe that unreconciled relationships are the norm—part of "reality" in the fallen order that will be undone only when Christ returns.

To be sure, full redemption will take place only when Christ returns and heaven and earth are renewed. Nevertheless, until that time followers of Christ, who have been reconciled to God through Christ, are called to serve as agents of reconciliation. In his Letter to the Romans, Paul discusses the marks of true faith. Among other things, he highlights the quality of pursuing peace: "Live in harmony with one another. Do not be haughty . . . Repay no one evil for evil, but give thought to do what is honorable in the sight of all. If possible, so far as it depends on you, live peaceably with all" (Rom 12:16–18). We need to come to terms with the fact that we are neglecting our basic Christian duty and character.

Moreover, it's helpful to think "big picture." In the short run, it may seem like our ministry efforts at the cost of reconciliation are yielding fruit. We see people coming to faith through our many programs. Yet, what happens in the long-run? Perhaps some individuals were netted in through a fun student program or a robust Men's Ministry. As they join the community, they go through a honeymoon period. But then they experience conflict—either directly or indirectly—and they experience the contradiction: by grace we have been received into the family of God; however, we refuse to be reconciled and receive our own enemies, even those who profess to be part of the same family. Eventually the dissonance overwhelms and those same converts leave, turned off by the hypocrisy of those who have been forgiven much.[1] We just do not appreciate enough the long-term impact of unreconciled relationships.

On the flip side, there is much to be gained—deep and lasting good—when we commit to creating a new norm, when we seek to become peacemakers and foster a culture of peace. Sande relates this simple but powerful illustration:

> When I was in law school, I brought a friend to church. Cindy was struggling in her spiritual life and disillusioned with her church. Thinking she might benefit from my church, I had invited her to worship with me one Sunday.
>
> Moments after we took our seats, Pastor Erbele surprised everyone. He called for the attention of the congregation and asked one of the elders to come forward. Suddenly I remembered that these two men had had a heated discussion during the previous week's Sunday school class . . .
>
> Pastor Erbele put his arm around Kent's shoulders and went on. "We want you to know that we met later

1. An example of this is seen with novelist Anne Rice. Once an atheist, she converted to Christianity; a few years later, she said this: "Today I quit being a Christian. I'm out. I remain committed to Christ as always but not to being 'Christian' or to being part of Christianity. It's simply impossible for me to 'belong' to this quarrelsome, hostile, disputatious, and deservedly infamous group" ("Reason for Quitting Christianity").

that afternoon to resolve our differences. By God's grace, we came to understand each other better, and we were fully reconciled. But we need to tell you how sorry we are for disrupting the unity of this fellowship, and we ask for your forgiveness for the poor example we gave last week."

. . . The rest of the service was a blur, and before long I was driving her home. We made light conversation for a few minutes, but eventually Cindy referred to what had happened: "I still can't believe what your pastor did this morning. I've never seen a minister do something like that. Could I come back next week?"

During the subsequent weeks, Cindy listened intently when my pastor spoke. Having seen the power of the gospel in his life, she was eager to hear about the salvation and freedom she could experience by trusting in Jesus. Within a month, she committed her life to Christ and made our church her spiritual home.[2]

While there isn't a single way for people to come to faith, it appears that the love believers have for one another, expressed especially in reconciliation, should be so attractive that the gospel will win an audience with many. Perhaps when the pursuit of reconciliation becomes a revived norm in the church, we will see many conversions not unlike Cindy's.

"The grace of the Lord Jesus Christ be with your spirit" (v. 25) as you seek to create cultures of reconciliation.

2. Sande, *Peacemaker*, 49–50.

Appendix

Translation and Notes[1]

1 PAUL, PRISONER[2] FOR Christ Jesus, and Timothy the brother. To Philemon our beloved fellow worker[3] 2 and Apphia our sister and Archippus our fellow soldier, and the church according to your

---

1. The *English Standard Version* (*ESV*) offers a very fine translation of the Letter to Philemon. The following is my own translation of the Greek text. I have provided it here for the purpose of highlighting certain linguistic and rhetorical features of the letter. My translation will sound a bit more "wooden" at times, but I assume the reader has access to much more readable versions of the letter.

2. Notable is the use of "prisoner" instead of "apostle," which is Paul's more regular self-identification. There are at least several reasons for this: Paul wants to identify with the "lowly" Onesimus; he wants Philemon to feel compassion for him in his imprisoned state; and he wants to make clear that he is ultimately under the rule of God, that is, he is not a prisoner because of Caesar's reign but because of God's sovereignty.

3. Though Paul also names Apphia and Archippus (possibly Philemon's wife and son, respectively [see e.g., Lightfoot, *Colossians and Philemon*, 131]) and "the church in your house" (*ESV*), the context of the letter makes clear that Philemon is the primary addressee. Also, as Moo observes, "the pattern of ancient letters was to list the primary addressee first, and this points to Philemon" (*Letters*, 362).

house:[4] 3 Grace to you and peace from God our Father and the Lord Jesus Christ.[5]

4 I thank my[6] God always when I remember you in my prayers, 5 because I hear of your love and of the faith that you have toward the Lord Jesus and for all the saints,[7] 6 and I pray that the

---

4. It is almost impossible to miss the familial and fellowship imagery permeating these two verses. Timothy is a "brother" and Apphia is a "sister." The Greek preposition *sun*, which is translated in the *ESV* as "fellow" is used to modify Philemon's status as a "fellow worker" and Archippus as a "fellow soldier." Also, the believers with Philemon are specified as "the church according to your house." This is an obvious reference to the reality of "house-churches." But it also reiterates the household and familial picture that Paul is depicting in all the opening identifiers. Finally, there is the repeated use of "our" to convey that the senders and recipients of the letter are one in Christ. The apostle is clearly orienting Philemon and the believers with him to hear all the words that follow in this letter in the context of family and intimate fellowship. It is not by accident that Wright considers "fellowship" the central theme of Philemon: "It is a letter which, at one level 'about' *koinōnia*, Christian fellowship and mutual participation, is at a far deeper level an outworking, in practice, of that principle" (*Epistles*, 170)

5. The terms "grace" and "peace" remind Philemon and all the secondary recipients of the era of "grace" and "peace" into which God has brought them in Christ. First and foremost, they have received unmerited favor and now have peace with God. As such, they ought to be agents of grace and peace in the lives of others, especially among those who profess faith in Christ.

Several times in this brief letter there are references to prayer (6, 22; cf. 3). While each does not deal directly with reconciliation, the frequency of prayer reminds us of the critical role prayer plays in reconciliation. In many cases, the problem is not ignorance—it's not as though two spouses do not know they should stop with the silent treatment and pursue peace. Rather, with conflict there is a profound hardness of heart that requires a supernatural softening. While there are important steps we must take to facilitate reconciliation, we must also recognize that reconciliation represents a supernatural work of the Lord.

6. Though Timothy is listed as a co-author, Paul says here, "I thank *my* God." This reflects the somewhat "private" quality of the letter, though our understanding of "private" is likely different from the way the apostle would have thought of it (see Moo, *Letters*, 362–63). Though others are listed as the recipients, in one sense the letter expresses a personal matter between Paul and Philemon (and Onesimus). By narrowing the focus in this way, the force of Paul's words becomes stronger: Philemon is not heeding a general exhortation to extend mercy but—much more—a personal one from his beloved friend, the apostle Paul.

7. It is worth noting that reconciliation was hard even for a man as godly as Philemon, who displayed tangible love for the saints and faith in the Lord Jesus. What illustrates this is the fact that Philemon seems exceedingly generous.

fellowship[8] of your faith may become effective for the full knowledge of every good thing that is in us for the sake of Christ.[9] 7 For I have derived much joy and comfort from your love because the hearts of the saints have been refreshed through you,[10] brother.[11]

8 Accordingly, though I am bold enough in Christ to command you to do what is required,[12] 9 yet for love's sake I prefer

---

Many Christians struggle with generosity—as I often say, "Money makes us funny." Philemon seems to have transcended this struggle common among many believers. Yet, he seems to fall short in the area of reconciliation. There seems to be something uniquely challenging about the work of reconciliation.

8. The Greek term translated "sharing" (*ESV*) is *koinōnia*," which means "fellowship." This reiterates the theme of fellowship that we see in the opening verses of the letter; thus the translation, "the fellowship of your faith."

9. A survey of commentaries reflects the challenges involved in interpreting verse 6. Moo's paraphrase is helpful: "Philemon, I am praying that the mutual participation that arises from your faith in Christ might become effective in leading you to understand and put into practice all the good that God wills for us and that is found in our community; and do all this for the sake of Christ" (*Letters*, 394).

10. Concerning verses 4–7, we know that Paul's intention in writing this letter is to facilitate reconciliation between Onesimus and Philemon. As Paul notes in verse 8, he has the authority to command peace. Yet, he chooses an indirect route, namely that of relationship and communication, rather than the more "efficient" route of giving orders.

Reconciliation between two parties will often require the intervention of another party. This outside party usually has a positive relationship with the two parties in consideration and therefore is in a unique position to facilitate reconciliation. However, this third party should be deliberate and winsome in his or her speech and approach, as Paul exemplifies in this letter.

11. Contra most English translations, I note here how verse 7 in Greek concludes with the direct reference to Philemon as "brother." In Paul's letters, "brothers" (plural) refers to all believers, male and female. Here, the singular form "brother" focuses on the personal relationship between Paul and Philemon. In addition, its placement at the end of verse 7 and immediately before the body of the letter sets the stage for the personal and familial request Paul is about to make of Philemon concerning Onesimus.

12. The phrase "to do what is required" is instructive. Though the Letter to Philemon is an appeal, the substance of what Paul is requesting—reconciliation—is "required" of all believers. We forget that reconciliation is at the heart of the gospel and that we are mandated to forgive as God has forgiven us in Christ Jesus.

to appeal to you[13]—I, Paul, an old man and now a prisoner also for Christ Jesus—[14] 10 I appeal to you for my child, Onesimus, whom I begat in my imprisonment. 11 (Formerly he was useless to you, but now he is indeed useful to you and to me.)[15] 12 I have sent him back to you, that is, I have sent back my very heart.[16] 13 I would have preferred to keep him for myself, in order that he might serve me on your behalf during my imprisonment for the gospel,[17] 14 but I wished to do nothing without your own resolve, in order that your goodness might not be according to compul-

13. Wright's comments here are worth noting: "Behind this choice of the right sort of appeal lies an all-important point: living Christianly makes people more human, not less. No Christian should grumble at extra demands of love. They are golden opportunities to draw on the reserves of divine love, and in so doing to become more fully oneself in Christ, more completely in the image of God, more authentically human" (*Epistles*, 18).

14. Some might argue that Paul is being manipulative here by drawing attention to his age and status. I would argue that Paul is seeking to bring about sobriety. When we are angry, our outlook on the world becomes warped: we literally stop seeing clearly. By reminding Philemon of his own imprisonment for the gospel, Paul is trying to break Philemon from the shackles of anger and awaken him to the reality that our greatest and highest calling is to live in step with the gospel for the sake of Christ.

15. Noteworthy is Paul's use of "formerly . . . but now" language. This sort of language underscores the significance of conversion: a person can no longer view him or herself the same way post-conversion. Similarly, other believers can no longer view him or her in the same way. Developing this new perspective is integral for facilitating the work of reconciliation.

16. What is Paul doing here (and in v. 10)? He is reshaping the way Philemon views Onesimus. Currently, Onesimus is nothing but a perpetrator of evil in the eyes of Philemon. He is someone that has wronged his former master. Yet, Paul is inviting Philemon to look at this troublemaker through new eyes in order to facilitate reconciliation. Specifically, Paul wants Philemon to view Onesimus in light of Paul: Onesimus is Paul's spiritual "child"—his very "heart." The rhetorical impact of these identifiers is obvious: for Philemon to continue to refuse fellowship with Onesimus is akin to a personal affront to Paul himself.

17. The contrast here is obvious and significant. On the one hand, Paul indicates clearly what he would have preferred. Still, he surrenders his preferences for Philemon's sake. In doing so, he models what he will soon ask of Philemon—the surrender of his rights (what is owed to him) for Onesimus's sake and for the sake of making peace.

sion but according to conviction.[18] 15 For perhaps this is why he was separated from you for a brief period,[19] that you might have him back forever,[20] 16 no longer as a bondservant but more than a bondservant, as a beloved brother—especially to me, but how much more to you, both in the flesh and in the Lord.[21] 17 So if you hold me as your fellowship partner,[22] receive him as you would receive me.[23] 18 If he has wronged you at all, or owes you anything,

18. Here we have another contrast: "compulsion" versus "conviction." In the end, Paul wants Philemon to reconcile out of a personal decision, not because of an obligation imposed on him. This verse reminds us that reconciliation will often depend less on positive feelings or a change on our enemy's part and more on our resolve to obey God's call to forgive our enemies as he has forgiven us in Christ.

19. On Paul's use of "perhaps," Wright comments (*Epistles*, 184): "In this process, of attempting to understand a situation from God's point of view and so responding to it in a Christian fashion, there is always room for restrained speculation about the providential purpose that may underlie curious events. If it is true that 'in all things God works for the good of those who love him' (Rom. 8:28), it is also true that Christians are sometimes, and to a limited extent, privileged to catch a glimpse of how this is being accomplished."

20. Here, again, we have another contrast: a "brief period" versus "forever." Paul wants Philemon to adopt an "eternal perspective" on the situation. He is caught in the moment, focused solely on how Onesimus has hurt him. It is not so much that Paul is minimizing Philemon's pain, but he wants Philemon to remember that he is an eternal person engaging another eternal person with eternity at stake (C. S. Lewis gets at this point in *Weight of Glory*, 45–46). Paul is convinced that Philemon will become more sober about the situation when he adopts the perspective of eternity.

21. There can be no question that the gospel makes life more complicated because salvation involves adoption: in Christ we become members of God's household. This means we are now family with people who were previously not our brothers and sisters. Thus, life inevitably becomes more complicated with the mix of "family and business."

Even though Paul does not make an explicit request, it is possible that Paul is hoping that Philemon—on his own accord—would decide to free Onesimus given his new status as a "beloved brother" in the faith. Doing so would be an outworking of Paul's prayer in verse 6, that Philemon would discern every good work as he lives in fellowship with other believers.

22. See verse 6 for notes on the significance of "fellowship."

23. Reconciliation is more than coexistence—it's an embrace of our enemies. Paul sets high standards: "receive him as you would receive me."

charge that to my account.[24] 19 I, Paul, write this with my own hand: I will repay it—to say nothing of your owing me even your own self.[25] 20 Yes, brother, I want some benefit from you in the Lord. Refresh my heart in Christ.[26] 21 Confident of your obedience, I write to you, knowing that you will do even more than I say. 22 At the same time, prepare a guest room for me, for I am hoping that through your prayers I will be graciously given to you. 23 Epaphras, my fellow prisoner in Christ Jesus, sends greetings to you, 24 and so do Mark, Aristarchus, Demas, and Luke, my fellow workers. 25 The grace of the Lord Jesus Christ be with your spirit.[27]

24. The conditional quality of Paul's statement ("if . . .") suggests that he neither assumed Onesimus's guilt nor denied it. This ambiguous statement suggests that Paul was more concerned about facilitating reconciliation than assigning guilt. Dunn observes, "it neatly serves the purpose of taking for granted Philemon's view that Onesimus was guilty of [a] serious misdemeanor, without wholly conceding that Philemon's judgment was entirely correct" (*Epistles*, 338).

25. Paul's basic message to Philemon: "You owe me." Onesimus is not the only (supposed) debtor.

26. Wright, *Epistles*, 188–89: "This translation scarcely catches the mood of the Greek, which might perhaps be expressed: 'Yes, my dear man—now I come to think of it, *I* want some return from *you!*' . . . The 'my' is emphatic in the Greek: it is now *my* turn to be refreshed. How? By Philemon welcoming (not Paul, but) Onesimus: the principle of *koinōnia* is at work still."

27. Moo, *Letters*, 422: "Since this grace wish is so much a staple of Paul's letter closings, it might be that he adds it here without giving it much thought. But we might wonder whether Paul could ever write about grace without thinking about its significance. And here he might especially be aware of how much the whole community would need a strong measure of grace in order to respond well to the Onesimus affair." Similarly, Wright, *Epistles*, 192: "The conventional tone of the closing greeting, once again, should not blind us to the truth it conveys to us, and the power that the expressed prayer conveyed to Philemon. It is a hard thing Paul has asked of him: a superhuman task of heartfelt reconciliation and forgiveness. If he is to do it without pride or anger, he cannot do it without grace."

Bibliography

Barth, Markus, and Helmut Blanke. *The Letter to Philemon: A New Translation with Notes and Commentary*. Eerdmans Critical Commentary. Grand Rapids: Eerdmans, 2000.

Batten, Alicia J. "Philemon." In *Philippians, Colossians, Philemon*, edited by Mary Ann Beavis, 201–264. Wisdom Commentary 51. Collegeville, MN: Liturgical, 2017.

Blair, Leonardo. "Tim Keller Warns Christians About Being Divided by Politics: 'You're Christian First.'" *The Christian Post*. October 28, 2016. https://www.christianpost.com/news/tim-keller-warns-christians-about-being-divided-by-politics-youre-christian-first-171157/?m=1. Accessed March 20, 2018.

Bridges, Jerry. *Respectable Sins: Confronting the Sins We Tolerate*. Colorado Springs, CO: NavPress, 2007.

Burtchaell, James Tunstead. *Philemon's Problem: A Theology of Grace*. Grand Rapids: Eerdmans, 1998.

Byers, Ann. *Jeff Bezos: The Founder of Amazon.com*. Internet Career Biographies. New York: Rosen, 2007.

Cochran, Jeff L., and Nancy H. Cochran. *The Heart of Counseling: Counseling Skills Through Therapeutic Relationships*. Second edition. New York: Routledge, 2015.

Colvin, Geoff. *Talent Is Overrated: What Really Separates World-Class Performers from Everybody Else*. New York, Portfolio, 2010.

———. "Talent is Overrated Author GEOFF COLVIN: The Myth of Hard Work & Natural Talent." March 15, 2012. https://www.youtube.com/watch?v=ifmjfvhM3fA. Accessed April 26, 2018.

DeYmaz, Mark, and Harry Li. *Ethnic Blends: Mixing Diversity into Your Local Church*. Leadership Network Innovation Series. Grand Rapids: Zondervan, 2010.

Dunn, James D. G. *The Epistles to the Colossians and to Philemon: A Commentary on the Greek Text*. Grand Rapids: Eerdmans, 1996.

Edwards, Jonathan. *The Works of Jonathan Edwards, Vol. 1*. Carlisle, PA: The Banner of Truth Trust, 1979.

Ezigbo, Victor I. *Introducing Christian Theologies: Voices from Global Christian Communities, Vol. 2.* Eugene, OR: Cascade, 2015.

Gaffin Jr., Richard B. *By Faith, Not by Sight: Paul and the Order of Salvation.* Second edition. Phillipsburg, NJ: P&R, 2013.

Garces-Foley, Kathleen. *Crossing the Ethnic Divide: The Multiethnic Church on a Mission.* New York: Oxford University Press, 2007.

Gray, Peter. *Psychology.* Fourth edition. New York: Worth, 2002.

Haase, Albert. *Coming Home to Your True Self: Leaving the Emptiness of False Attractions.* Downers Grove, IL: InterVarsity, 2008.

Harrington, Daniel J. *Paul's Prison Letters: Spiritual Commentaries on Paul's Letters to Philemon, the Philippians, and the Colossians.* Hyde Park, NJ: New City, 1997.

Hart, Kevin, with Neil Strauss. *I Can't Make This Up: Life Lessons.* New York: 37 INK/Atria, 2017.

Heil, John Paul. "The Chiastic Structures of Philemon." *Biblica* 82.2 (2001) 178–206.

Hooker, Morna D. "A Partner in the Gospel: Paul's Understanding of His Ministry." In *Theology and Ethics in Paul and His Interpreters: Essays in Honor of Victor Paul Furnish,* edited by Earnest H. Lovering Jr. and Jerry I. Sumney, 83–100. Nashville, TN: Abingdon, 1996.

Horton, Michael. *Ordinary: Sustainable Faith in a Radical, Restless World.* Grand Rapids: Zondervan, 2014.

Isaacson, Walter. *Steve Jobs.* New York: Simon & Schuster, 2011.

Jeon, Paul S. *1 Timothy: A Charge to God's Missional Household, Vol. 1.* Eugene, OR: Pickwick, 2017.

———. *1 Timothy: A Charge to God's Missional Household, Vol. 3.* Eugene, OR: Pickwick, 2017.

———. *A New King: Encountering the Risen Son.* Eugene, OR: Wipf & Stock, 2018.

———. *True Faith: Reflections on Paul's Letter to Titus.* Eugene, OR: Wipf & Stock, 2012.

Johnson, Rian. *Star Wars: The Last Jedi.* Directed by Rian Johnson. Walt Disney Studios Motion Pictures, 2017.

Katongole, Emmanuel, and Chris Rice. *Reconciling All Things: A Christian Vision for Justice, Peace, and Healing.* Downers Grove, IL: InterVarsity, 2008.

Kellemen, Robert W. *Gospel-Centered Counseling: How Christ Changes Lives.* Equipping Biblical Counselors. Grand Rapids: Eerdmans, 2014.

Keller, Timothy. *Center Church: Doing Balanced, Gospel-Centered Ministry in Your City.* Grand Rapids: Zondervan, 2012.

———. "Excerpts from a Sermon: Gospel-Centered Ministry: 1 Peter 1:1–12 and 1:22—2:12." *The Spurgeon Fellowship Journal* (2008). www.reformedontheweb.com/gospelcentered-keller.pdf. Accessed March 2, 2018.

————. *The Freedom of Self-Forgetfulness: The Path to True Christian Joy.* UK: 10Publishing, 2013.

————. *Making Sense of God: An Invitation for the Skeptical.* New York: Viking, 2016.

————. *Ministries of Mercy: The Call of the Jericho Road.* Third edition. Phillipsburg, NJ: P&R, 2015.

Klein, William W. *The New Chosen People: A Corporate View of Election.* Revised and Expanded Edition. Eugene, OR: Wipf & Stock, 2015.

Kwon, Duke. "Jesus and Your Political Party." *The Witness: A Black Christian Collective.* October 25, 2016. https://thewitnessbcc.com/jesus-political-party/. Accessed March 20, 2018.

Larson, Duane H. "Life Together Is Only in God: The Achievement of Personhood in Community." In *The Difficult but Indispensable Church*, edited by Norma Cook Everist, 13–22. Minneapolis, MN: Fortress, 2002.

Lewis, C. S. *The Chronicles of Narnia, Vol. 1: The Lion, the Witch, and the Wardrobe.* Hong Kong: Enrich Spot, 2016.

————. *The Four Loves.* New York: Harcourt Brace & Company, 1988.

————. *The Weight of Glory.* New York: HarperOne, 1976.

Lightfoot, J. B. *Colossians and Philemon.* The Crossway Classic Commentaries. Wheaton, IL: Crossway, 1997.

Longenecker, Bruce W. "Philemon." In *Philippians and Philemon*, James W. Thompson and Bruce W. Longenecker, 149–196. Paideia: Commentaries on the New Testament. Grand Rapids: Baker Academic, 2016.

Love, Rick. *Peace Catalysts: Resolving Conflict in Our Families, Organizations, and Communities.* Downers Grove, IL: InterVarsity, 2014.

MacArthur, John. *Colossians & Philemon.* The MacArthur New Testament Commentary. Chicago, IL: Moody, 1992.

Malphurs, Aubrey. *The Nuts and Bolts of Church Planting: A Guide for Starting Any Kind of Church.* Grand Rapids: Baker, 2011.

McKinley, Mike. *Am I Really a Christian?* Wheaton, IL: Crossway, 2011.

Migliore, Daniel L. *Philippians and Philemon.* Belief: A Theological Commentary on the Bible. Louisville, KY: Westminster John Knox, 2014

Mishra, Braj Kumar. *Psychology: The Study of Human Behaviour.* Second edition. Delhi: PHI Learning, 2016.

Moo, Douglas J. *The Letters to the Colossians and to Philemon.* Grand Rapids: Eerdmans, 2008.

Murray, John. *The Imputation of Adam's Sin.* Phillipsburg, NJ: P&R, 1959.

Parker, T. H. L. *Calvin's New Testament Commentaries.* Second edition. Louisville, KY: Westminster John Knox, 1993.

Peterson, Norman R. *Rediscovering Paul: Philemon and the Sociology of Paul's Narrative World.* Eugene, OR: Wipf & Stock, 1985.

Piper, John. *Let the Nations Be Glad!: The Supremacy of God in Missions.* Third edition. Grand Rapids: Baker Academic, 2010.

Rice, Anne. "Reason for Quitting Christianity." *Anne Rice: The Official Site.* http://annerice.com/Chamber-Christianity.html. Accessed April 25, 2018.

Roth, Eric. *Forrest Gump*. Directed by Robert Zemeckis. Paramount Pictures, 1994.

Ryle, J. C. "Train Up a Child in the Way He Should Go: A Sermon for Parents: Preached in Helmingham Church, August 20, 1845." London: Seeley & Co., 1846.

Sager, Mike. "Kobe Bryant Doesn't Want Your Love." *Esquire*. November 29, 2015. https://www.esquire.com/sports/a3588/kobebryant1107/. Accessed March 1, 2018.

Sande, Ken. *The Peacemaker: A Biblical Guide to Resolving Personal Conflict*. Third edition. Grand Rapids: Baker, 2004.

Schweitzer, Don. *Jesus Christ for Contemporary Life: His Person, Work, and Relationships*. Eugene, OR: Cascade, 2012.

Snobelen, Stephen D. "The Biblical View of Nature." In *Science, Religion, and Society: An Encyclopedia of History, Culture, and Controversy, Vol. 1-2*, edited by Arri Eisen and Gary Laderman, 338–349. New York: Routledge, 2015.

Still, Todd D. *Philippians & Philemon*. Smyth & Helwys Bible Commentary 27b. Macon, GA: Smyth & Helwys, 2011.

Swoboda, A. J. "The Cross Creates a Paradox – Dr. A.J. Swoboda." Sermon. February 26, 2012. https://youtu.be/ytod5k_8k38. Accessed January 1, 2018.

Taylor, Charles. *The Ethics of Authenticity*. Cambridge, MA: Harvard University Press, 1991.

Tripp, Paul David. *Dangerous Calling: Confronting the Unique Challenges of Pastoral Ministry*. Wheaton, IL: Crossway, 2012.

———. *Parenting: 14 Gospel Principles that Can Radically Change Your Family*. Wheaton, IL: Crossway, 2016.

Van Yperen, Jim. *Making Peace: A Guide to Overcoming Church Conflict*. Chicago, IL: Moody, 2002.

Webber, Robert E. *Worship: Old & New*. Revised edition. Grand Rapids: Zondervan, 1994.

Wigg-Stevenson, Tyler. *The World Is Not Ours To Save: Finding the Freedom to Do Good*. Downers Grove, IL: InterVarsity, 2013.

Williams, Scott. *Church Diversity: Sunday: The Most Segregated Day of the Week*. Green Forest, AR: New Leaf, 2011.

Wilson, Timothy D., and Nancy Brekke. "Mental Contamination and Mental Correction: Unwanted Influences on Judgments and Evaluations." *Psychological Bulletin* 116.1 (1994) 117–42.

Witherington III, Ben. *The Letters to Philemon, the Colossians, and the Ephesians: A Socio-Rhetorical Commentary on the Captivity Epistles*. Grand Rapids: Eerdmans, 2007.

Wright, N. T. *The Epistles of Paul to the Colossians and to Philemon: An Introduction and Commentary*. The Tyndale New Testament Commentaries. Grand Rapids: Eerdmans, 1986.

Zempel, Heather. *Community Is Messy: The Perils and Promise of Small Group Ministry*. Downers Grove, IL: InterVarsity, 2012.

www.ingramcontent.com/pod-product-compliance
Lightning Source LLC
Chambersburg PA
CBHW071108090426
42737CB00013B/2537